“F

THE BRISTOL BRIDGE MASSACRE *of* 1793

Michael Manson

TANGENT BOOKS

Unit 5.16 Paintworks, Arnos Vale, Bristol BS4 3EH

RIOT! The Bristol Bridge Massacre of 1793 first published by Past & Present Press in 1997 (0-9532082-0-6). Second edition (978-1-909446-00-7) published by Bristol Books 2013. This edition published by Tangent Books 2016.

ISBN 978-1-910089-45-3

Design: Joe Burt (joe@wildsparkdesign.com)

A CIP record for this book is available from the British Library.

Printed on paper from a sustainable source.

Contents

Bibliographical Abbreviations

B.R.O.	Bristol Record Office.
B.R.L.	Bristol Reference Library.
F.F.J.	Felix Farley's Bristol Journal.
Latimer	Latimer, J., Annals of eighteenth century Bristol, (1893).
Matthews	Matthews, W., The New History of Bristol or the Complete Guide and Bristol Directory (1794).
Rose	Rose, J., An Impartial History of the Late Disturbances in Bristol, (1793).
Rosser	Anon., An Impartial History of the Late Riots in Bristol, (1793).
Committee	Minutes of the Committee for Investigating the Bridge Affairs, Bristol Reference Library B.13065.

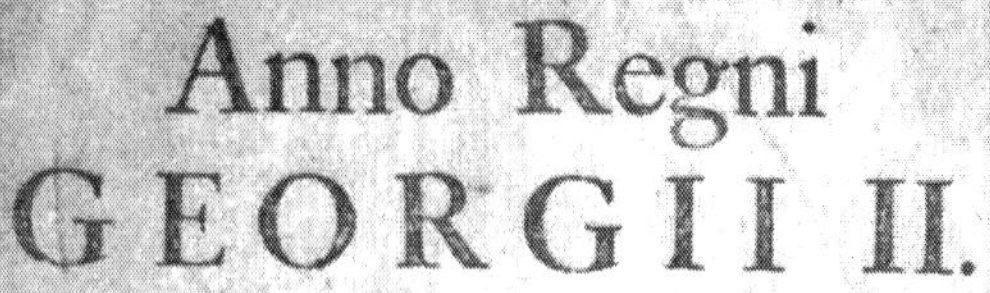

Anno Regni

GEORGII II.

REGIS

Magnæ Britanniæ, Franciæ, & Hiberniæ,

TRICESIMO TERTIO.

At the Parliament begun and holden at *Westminster*, the Thirty first Day of *May*, *Anno Dom.* 1754, in the Twenty seventh Year of the Reign of our Sovereign Lord *GEORGE* the Second, by the Grace of God, of *Great Britain*, *France*, and *Ireland*, King, Defender of the Faith, *&c.*

And from thence continued by several Prorogations to the Thirteenth Day of *November*, 1759, being the Seventh Session of this present Parliament.

LONDON:

Printed by *Thomas Baskett*, Printer to the King's most Excellent Majesty; and by the Assigns of *Robert Baskett*. 1760.

The Bristol Bridge Act of 1757. The Act lit a slow burning fuse that would set off a ferocious explosion 26 years later. (Bristol Reference Library)

Preface

For many Bristolians 1793 was turning out to be a difficult year. Inflation was increasing, trade was in decline, banks were in a state of crisis and jobs were scarce. On 1 February these problems were further exacerbated by the French Convention declaring war on Great Britain and Holland.

Among all these difficulties there was one seemingly small, but significant, piece of good news. At the end of September 1793 the Bristol Bridge toll, which had been a constant source of annoyance for 25 years, was due to cease. Or was it?

Introduction to the 1997 edition

'No, not THAT Bristol riot' has invariably been my response to those who have enquired about the subject of this book.

This is a book about the Bristol Bridge 'Riots' of 1793 – a dramatic and bloody series of events that have remained (with the exception of two notable studies) largely neglected and hidden in the darker reaches of Bristol's annals.

Do not, however, be put off by the 'riot's' obscurity. If one is to judge the significance of a riot by the number of people killed and injured, the troubles surrounding the collection of the Bristol Bridge toll in 1793 rank as one of the major civil disturbances of eighteenth century England. Indeed, the 'riot' could be seen to pinpoint 1793 as pivotal year in Bristol's history. It indicates the end of the city's golden age and the beginning – in comparison with the dynamic growth experienced by the cities of the north of England – of the slow decline of Bristol's fortunes.

Although Bristol has little radical tradition it has, paradoxically, an unenviable reputation for its riots. Today, many Bristolians are able to recite some of the mythology that surrounds the Bristol Riots of 1831. More recently, riots in the latter part of the twentieth century have left an indelible scar on local communities and the city's reputation in general.

One reason why the Bristol Bridge 'riots' have remained in the shadows for so long is the lack of comprehensive and robust documentary evidence. As will be explained, for a number of reasons – not all of them legitimate – there was no official inquiry into the disturbances. To build a picture of the events of 1793 I have had to sift through a range of official minutes, subjective reports, the minutes of an unofficial enquiry, newspapers, handbills, political ballads, lampoons, squibs and a whole range of other ephemera. There have been many pieces to the jigsaw; some of these pieces are warped – others are missing altogether.

Michael Manson
November 1997

Introduction to the 2016 edition

Massacre is an emotive term and not a particularly precise one. Its use has been historically controversial; indeed the events of September 1793 described in this book were presaged a quarter of a century earlier by a remarkably similar controversy and in similar circumstances. At issue in 1768 was the killing of at least 12 unarmed supporters of the radical agitator John Wilkes by soldiers in St George's Fields, London. Magistrates ordered a dispersal, the Riot Act was read, mud and stones were thrown and troops opened fire – ostensibly over the heads of the crowd, but the resulting carnage told its own story. Wilkes swiftly dubbed the slayings a massacre and government ministers countered by denying they were anything of the sort. 'If not a massacre, by what other name then shall we call it?', demanded Wilkes. 'Shall we, with the smooth-tongued Secretary at War, call it merely a *disagreeable circumstance*?' [1] Similarly semantic arguments were rehearsed over Peterloo in 1819, a quarter of a century after the events on Bristol Bridge. Indeed, as Peterloo's most recent historian has noted, these are arguments still not entirely laid to rest. Although for E. P. Thompson, 'it really was a massacre', instigated clearly enough by 'class hatred', some later analysts have preferred the more equivocal terms 'incident' or 'tragedy'. [2]

The problem, of course, is a political one, for to boldly state that soldiers acting under the authority of local or national government were suffered to use deadly force on unarmed civilians is tantamount to an accusation of conspiracy to murder. Massacre may elude precise definition but its inference is not a conflict or a battle but an uneven act of pitiless destruction and arbitrary power. 'On the night between', one satire of 1793 had a Bristol magistrate reflecting without remorse, 'we cruelly caused to be mowed down many innocent persons'.[3] And in its insistence on the indiscriminate murder of the innocent, it is a phrase that speaks the language of massacre. In Wilkes's estimation, whatever word government liked to use for the St George's Fields affair, if justice were not done on behalf of its innocent victims, 'it may perhaps prove the cause of still more *disagreeable circumstances*'.[4] And whilst English magistrates were more loathe than ever after that to deploy soldiers as a peacekeeping force, the very infrequency of their use made it all the more devastating. Time would prove Wilkes right. Although independent coroners found a number of cases of homicide to answer, and several soldiers and even a magistrate were put to the bar for murder, there were no convictions and the efforts of Edmund Burke and others to have a full enquiry established came to nothing. A similar pattern would follow at Bristol in 1793, just as it followed Peterloo in 1819.[5]

Whether to regard the 'disagreeable circumstances' on Bristol Bridge as a massacre, a riot or an unfortunate tragedy, readers may decide for themselves after digesting the detail of this book. The 1790s were a decade in which the word 'massacre' was bandied around in unprecedented ways and with unprecedented frequency, a reflection of the much bloodier events taking place simultaneously in Revolutionary France, where it was appropriated even for the execution of the King and Queen. [6] Critics of Bristol Corporation were, unsurprisingly, anxious to inflict adversarial wounds. 'The killed and wounded on this fatal day amounted to upwards of seventy', wrote the radical young poet Robert Lovell in 1794, 'their names will remain an eternal monument to the infamy of those who ordered the Militia to fire; and to the disgrace of the inhabitants of this city, who have neglected to support an investigation of the cause of so horrid a massacre'.[7]

The story you are about to read in this well researched and very accessible account is not as well known as it deserves to be, either in Bristol or further afield. Robert Lovell's claim that there were more than 70 casualties may have been exaggerated but 63 were identified in the immediate aftermath – rather more than at St George's Fields if considerably fewer than the 654 killed or wounded at Peterloo. Either side of Peterloo, military intervention would claim the lives of some 300 Londoners during the Gordon Riots in 1780 (there are no reliable figures for the number of wounded survivors) and of an incalculable number at Bristol once again during the reform riots of 1831. The Home Office did its best to find out but as one commanding officer explained, 'I can give no idea... everything was done at a gallop and with the sword and in consequence for one that was killed, a hundred were wounded'. Another admitted his men had pursued unknown numbers of people to their deaths in burning buildings. 'I have reason to think the numbers of killed and wounded by the Dragoons, which I estimated in a former letter at 400 is considerably under the truth', he advised. 'So many killed have been ascertained, that the usual proportion of wounded, especially in an 'arms blanche' business, would amount almost to double that number'.[8] However, the Gordon Riots and the Bristol Reform Riots are considerably better known events than the massacre on Bristol Bridge. Given that they also involved larger crowds, widespread looting and the firing and destruction of buildings while the Bridge 'riot' did not, the military response at the Bridge was certainly disproportionate. Without doubt, great numbers of those killed in 1780 and 1831 were not rioters but bystanders. This was also true of the Bridge; indeed we must stretch the meaning of 'riot' somewhat to ascribe it to the building of a couple of bonfires out of broken toll-booths – all the more reason, perhaps, for the Bridge massacre to be remembered.

While there are differences, there remain some interesting similarities. One thing we now know about Hanoverian crowds is that their 'riots' and protests were rarely indiscriminate or unrestrained. The crowds of 1780 and 1831 may have embarked on a course of material destruction, but they committed very little interpersonal violence despite access to arms, and their targets – mainly institutions of fiscal, judicial and ecclesiastical inequality – were not chosen at random. A single conviction drove the crowd on Bristol Bridge – that the resumption of tolls was legally and morally wrong. That the perceived avarice of the Bridge Trustees should place an unjustified tax on trade at a time when the whole city's economy was in deep recession only strengthened the case. Historians have been interested for some time in the extent to which all eighteenth century crowd disturbances were underpinned by a legal and moral 'legitimizing notion', strong enough to overcome customary levels of deference and sufficiently resolute to expect support from the institutions of authority. The idea was first applied by E. P. Thompson to crowd actions relating to the unjust and uncustomary marketing of essential foodstuffs – a 'moral economy'. Thompson was extremely cautious about stretching the term into other areas of social and economic life, and Mark Harrison has examined the case for a 'moral economy' of bridge tolls at Bristol and found it unconvincing.[9] Nevertheless, the readiness of a respectable Bristol crowd to obstruct the taking of tolls for a couple of days, to either assist in the firing of toll-booths or stand by while it happened, and to refuse to disperse when confronted by armed soldiers under the

Riot Act, invites some interesting questions about deference and notions of 'right'.

Equally, the inability of the Corporation's critics to bring anyone to book for the massacre, despite the findings of coroners inquests on the dead, speaks volumes about the unaccountable nature of eighteenth century local government. Bristol Corporation had clashed with coroners' juries before over the deaths of civilians during riots, although on previous occasions in 1730 and 1753, the dead were weavers and colliers from 'without the gate', and the perpetrators armed citizens rather than soldiers. In both cases, inquest findings of homicide were over-ruled by the mayor with the support of the Attorney General. Bringing a body as powerful and self-confident as Bristol Corporation to account was no easier in 1793 than it had been sixty years earlier.

Given the reluctance of the Corporation to report any details of the massacre to the Home Office, and their steadfast refusal to countenance a public inquiry, there were many in Bristol who feared the whole matter might yet be lost to future generations. 'However strange' noted one incredulous pamphleteer, 'it appears to be almost probable that the Facts and Merits of the late Disastrous Transactions are in danger of passing into oblivion without any proper Exertion to have them clearly ascertained and fully committed to record!'[10] There is still no memorial to the dead; no plaque marks the spot on Bristol Bridge. But this book is ample demonstration of our need to remember.

Steve Poole
Associate Professor of Social and Cultural History
University of the West of England, Bristol.

Notes

1. *The North Briton*, 63 (1769), p.378
2. For an excellent summary of the debate, see Robert Poole, 'By the Law or the Sword: Peterloo Revisited', *History*, 91, 302 (2006).
3. *The Speech of Alderman Twig Pigeon Concerning the Late Riot in Bristol* (Bristol, 1793), p5.
4. *The North Briton*, ibid.
5. Incidences of military intervention in civilian disturbances are well analysed in Tony Hater, *The Army and the Crowd in Mid-Georgian England* (Macmillan, 1978).
6. See for example the popular broadside, *Massacre of the French King: View of La Guillotine or the Modern Beheading Machine at Paris* (London, 1793).
7. Robert Lovell, *Bristol: A Satire* (Bristol, 1794).
8. For the Gordon Riots see, for instance, Adrian Randall, *Riotous Assemblies: Popular Protest in Hanoverian England* (Oxford University Press, 2006), p.203. The figures for Peterloo are taken from Michael Bush, *The Casualties of Peterloo* (Carnegie Publishing, Lancaster, 2005). For Bristol in 1831 see The National Archives, *Home Office Papers, HO 40/28*, memorandum of major William Beckwith, 2 November 1831 and Major Digby Mackworth to Lord Fitzroy Somerset, 4 November 1831.
9. Mark Harrison, *Crowds and History: Mass Phenomena in English Towns, 1790-1835* (Cambridge University Press, 1988), pp.271-288.
10. Veritas, *Inquisition for Blood Shall be Made: To the Inhabitants of Bristol and Parts Adjacent* (Bristol, 1793)

Acknowledgements

Historians researching Bristol's past are twice blessed. Not only do they have the resources of one of the country's leading local authority archives to plunder, but they also have access to the outstanding local collection maintained by the Central Bristol Reference Library. Furthermore the quality of these collections is matched by the dedicated, enthusiastic and knowledgable staff who care for them.

My profound gratitude to all those people who have helped me along the way. On the research side my thanks to: Dr Peter Fleming from the University of the West of England for initial interest in the idea; Dr Margaret Bonney, Editor of the Local Historian for bringing together my thoughts on Pamphlets and Broadsheets; Francis Greenacre of the Bristol City Museum and Art Gallery; Lieutenant Colonel T.J.B. Hill, official archivist for the Herefordshire Regiment; Sir Ian Gilmour for taking time to read the whole manuscript and for providing such encouragement; and the ever enthusiastic John Sansom who is responsible for the publication of so many admirable books on Bristol's history through Redcliffe Press. Lorraine Mullaney undertook the copy-editing. My sincere thanks to all of the above.

This project has taken more time than I ever imagined at the outset. Along the way numerous friends and family have invariably, and sometimes unwittingly, contributed. I owe a long-term debt to my dear friend Chris Challis who gave me the courage many years ago to first put pen to paper – you live on in our hearts and memories, Chris. Thanks go to: Chris Hayllar, who revived the cry 'Give 'em Bristol Bridge'; Maggie Moss who gave unceasing encouragement, support and made valiant attempts to stay awake while I read extracts to her; and finally to Hannah and Matthew Manson for access to the computer – sometimes!

Michael Manson, 1997

An unknown artist's impression of old Bristol Bridge. Built in 1274 the thoroughfare was so dark, cramped and busy that one could cross over the bridge without realising it. (Bristol Reference Library)

ONE

Bristol: narrow streets, narrow minds

Until the late 19th century Bristol Bridge carried the only road linking the north and south of the city – the next bridge crossing the Avon was six miles upstream at Keynsham. Old Bristol Bridge, built in 1247, was a four-arched medieval structure with some 30 ramshackle houses clinging to its sides and overhanging the water. The thoroughfare was so dark, cramped and busy that one could cross over the bridge without realising it. Indeed, the narrowness of the bridge – the roadway was only 14 feet wide – was a frequent source of complaint. (The editor of Daniel Defoe's Tour Thro' the Whole Island of Great Britain – the 1772 edition – had scathingly compared this narrowness with the minds of Bristolians![1] Yet for centuries the bridge was a vital element of the city's prosperity. Although there were five passenger ferries across the Avon (the fare was a halfpenny) anything that needed to be transported on wheels – or by sledge – had to go across the bridge[2].

The increase of traffic during the eighteenth century, brought about by the economic expansion of Bristol's golden age, put an obvious strain on the city's bridge and the surrounding streets. Throughout the day there was a constant queue of wagons, carts, carriages, geehoes (the local name for sledges), horses and livestock waiting to cross. For foot-passengers it could be dangerous; pedestrians could be pressed against the shop fronts as carts negotiated their way past each other. Limbs had been broken under carriage wheels.

The Bristol Bridge Act which authorised the construction of a new bridge to replace the old structure was passed by Parliament in November 1756. The Act specified that funds should be raised by a house rate, a toll on the bridge and a tax of two and a half pennies a ton on all ships coming into the port (except for certain coasters that paid by the voyage). The house tax was to be collected by the church wardens and overseers of the poor, while the ship money was to be collected by customs officials. The rate of toll on the bridge varied from one shilling for a loaded wagon drawn by six horses down to a halfpenny for a horse, mule or ass not drawing a carriage. Foot passengers, however, crossed without paying. In all, an expenditure of £12,000 was allowed by Parliament for the construction of the replacement bridge. The management of the bridge's affairs was vested in the Bridge Committee, consisting of 50 trustees. (Later, in 1778, when rumours of financial mismanagement were in circulation, the trustees farmed out the toll collection to a third party. The lease for this privilege was auctioned annually[3].)

Parliament knew that tolls were unpopular and would invariably meet with initial local resistance. Indeed, as we shall soon see, Bristol was notorious for the vociferousness of its population and the persuasiveness of its crowds. Only seven years before, in 1749, Bristol had been under-siege by an angry mob of several hundred people protesting against the turnpikes. The army was called in, and for a number of nights the city gates were closed at 10.00 pm. On this occasion the intimidation came to nothing and peace was soon restored[4]. Even so turnpike gates were a frequent target for arsonists.

Anticipating trouble, the Bristol Bridge Act specified that it was an offence to 'burn, set fire to, remove, pull down, cut down, pluck up or otherwise destroy or level any tollgate or tollhouse'. The penalty was straightforward: anyone found guilty of such a felony 'shall suffer death...without benefit of clergy'[5].

A NEW BRIDGE FOR BRISTOL

With the funding for the bridge settled the debate now moved onto the design. It was a long drawn-out process. The one point that was unanimously agreed was that it should be a bridge with a view - albeit a restricted and not particularly picturesque view. Bridges with houses on them were old-fashioned. (Though this did not stop the construction of Pulteney Bridge in Bath in 1770, the last habitable bridge to be built in England.)

The major point of discussion was whether to have a single

or multi-arched bridge. The first plan submitted by Bristol-based architect James Bridges was for a three arched structure with piers resting on the original medieval foundations. Rival plans – both bolder concepts featuring a single span – were put forward by John Wood the Younger from Bath and Ferdinando Stratford from Gloucester. In the end the debate focused as much on the personalities of the architects as it did on the merits of the design. John Wood the Younger powerfully promoted his pedigree; as son of the visionary architect responsible for the Circus in Bath and the Exchange in Bristol, he argued that his family's track record should carry the day.

Even after James Bridges had been awarded the contract, Wood and his supporters continued to denounce the winning design. (It was only a temporary setback to Wood's career; he went on to build, amongst others, the Royal Crescent in Bath, one of the most famous terraces in Europe.) Eventually, the pressure they exerted proved to be so intolerable that Bridges departed for the West Indies, with his work unfinished, never to return. Architect and stonemason Thomas Paty was left to oversee the completion of the work. As the architectural historian Walter Ison wrote, the process was an example of 'how private intrigue, public controversy and official procrastination could combine to impede the progress of an urgently needed improvement'[6].

As work neared completion a small number of enthusiasts vied for the honour of being the first to cross. Mr George Catcott, a well-known Bristol dilettante, paid the workmen five guineas for the distinction of being the first to ride over the bridge on horseback. 'On the 25 June 1767', wrote Catcott, 'the last stone was set in the centre-arch of Bristol Bridge at about six o'clock in the evening; and the next day, between seven and eight o'clock in the morning

I rode over a few loose planks which were placed on purpose'. The following year, George Weare, the outgoing Mayor, marked the end of his term in office by being the first person to go across the bridge in a carriage[7].

The new stone structure, with its understated classical elegance bearing more than just a passing resemblance to London's Westminster Bridge, was officially opened for foot passengers in 1768, and a year later for general traffic. For anyone crossing the bridge the most notable feature was the imposing seven foot high Portland stone balustrade designed to prevent livestock jumping into the Avon below. At last Bristol had its new bridge and the city had, for a while, cured its most pressing traffic problem. Nobody, however, could have predicted that this was to light a slow burning fuse that would set off a ferocious explosion 25 years later.

Notes

1. Marcy, P.T., Eighteenth Century Views of Bristol and Bristolians in Bristol in the eighteenth century ed. McGrath, P. (1972), p.29.
2. Bristol was well known for its transport by sledges – known locally as geehoes.
3. Mr. Seyer's Manuscripts relating to the History of Bristol, B.R.L. B.4533 p.41.
4. Manson, M., Bristol: Beyond the Bridge (1988), p. 52.
5. 'An act for rebuilding and enlarging the Bridge over the Avon (Bristol Bridge)", 33 Geo. 11 (13 November 1759), p.576, B.R.L. B11539.
6. Ison, W., The Georgian Buildings of Bristol (1952), p.114.
7. Evans, J., A Chronological Outline of the History of Bristol (1824), p.284.

THE MODERN BRIDGE.

Bearing more than just a passing resemblance to London's Westminster Bridge, the new Bristol Bridge was opened for general traffic in 1769. For a while Bristol had cured its most pressing traffic problem.

TWO

Bristol's 'Golden Age' loses its lustre

To fully understand the tragic events in Bristol during the autumn of 1793 it is necessary to give a brief introduction to some aspects of Bristol's economic, political and social life in the late eighteenth century.

In 1793 William Matthews, a printer from Broadmead, produced his first annual guide to Bristol. In epic tones the small volume presented the West Country capital as worthy of classical comparisons. It likened Bristol's hilly topography with the seven hills of Rome and compared the Avon to the 'Tyber in width, colour and rapidity'[1]. Matthews's Guide also perpetuated the boast that Bristol ranked in extent and population as second city in the Kingdom. It was a boast that was at least 40 years out of date. (Even more outrageous was the claim that Bristol was the sixth most populous city in Europe.)

In reality the 1790s was a decade of change for Bristol, and in many cases this was not a change for the better. The middle years of the eighteenth century have been called Bristol's 'golden age' – a time when its trade and industry expanded at an unprecedented rate. For many centuries Bristol had been an important seaport trading mainly with France, Ireland and the Iberian Peninsula. It was also a major centre for both coasting and inland trade – indeed boats with a shallow draft could sail up the River Severn to the Midlands. During the eighteenth century trade really took off with the growth of trans-Atlantic voyages. In 1687 240 ships cleared from Bristol; one hundred years later this figure had nearly doubled to 448.

In the same period the actual size of ships had quadrupled from about 20,000 tons to 76,000 tons[2]. While trade with Ireland was the mainstay of the port, it was the 'African Trade' that offered the opportunity for spectacular profits. The 'African Trade' is, of course, a euphemism for the notorious slave trade, a deeply hateful enterprise that Bristolians were to exploit in the most shameful manner. Although English merchants initially expressed a widespread revulsion of slavery, their lust for money eventually overcame their scruples[3]. For a brief period in the middle of the century Bristol dominated the trade. In 1755 it was recorded that 237 Bristol merchants were involved in the slave trade – it was said that the slave trade touched all aspects of the city's economy[4].

By the end of the century, however, Bristol's involvement had fallen sharply. In the nine years between 1795 and 1804 only

29 vessels sailed from Bristol to Africa[5]. There were a number of reasons for this. The plantations were now well established and largely self-sufficient in their requirements for forced labour. While they still relied on slaves for their workforce, there was little need to capture and transport Africans for this purpose. 'Not a negro has been purchased for my son's estate for a great many years', wrote the Bristol merchant, John Pinney, 'and the number, I believe is increased'[6]. In a way, the trade had gone full circle and it was the products of the plantations, sugar and tobacco, that now provided the basis of Bristol's overseas trade.

There was also a rising tide of opinion, spearheaded by the Quakers, that was beginning to question the morality of the trade. By the 1790s the horrors of the slave trade were a regular subject of discussion around the dinner tables of Bristol. John Wesley, a frequent visitor to Bristol, had repeatedly preached against the trade. Furthermore, a petition condemning it had been set up in February 1788 in the Guildhall. Evidence of slavery's atrocities was also gathered in Bristol by Thomas Clarkson to support William Wilberforce's anti-slavery bill of 1792. On the other hand, it must be said that Bristol's Society of Merchant Venturers was defiantly keen to safeguard the dwindling trade by setting up its own committee to protect the traffic. Even so 'Matthews' Directory' was able to proclaim that 'the ardour for the slave trade to Africa for men and women, our fellow creatures and equals is much abated among the humane and benevolent merchants of Bristol'[7]. Somewhat hypocritically, Matthews went on to point the finger at Bristol's rival port, saying that the merchants of Liverpool 'in their indiscriminate rage for commerce and getting money at all events, have newly engrossed this trade'

'AN INDUSTRIAL TOWN BEFORE THE INDUSTRIAL REVOLUTION'

While the foundations of Bristol's wealth lay in its trade and commerce, during the second half of the eighteenth century industry and manufacture became an increasingly important part of the city's economy. The main industries included glass, pottery, sugar and tobacco. The city's twelve glass houses made more glass than anywhere else in the country. They produced glass bottles used for Hotwell's Water, Cider, Perry and Wine, as well as window glass – much of which was exported to North America. The city's proximity to plentiful supplies of coal was an added stimulus to a number of local industries. All around the city the countryside was pockmarked by small 'bell pits'. Higher quality coal, used for domestic heating by those who could afford it, came from the Forest of Dean and could be bought by the ton from the quayside[8].

During the eighteenth century Bristol was at the forefront of a range of industrial innovation (though some of the industries only really thrived once they had moved elsewhere). Indeed, Bristol was, in the words of Bryan Little, 'an industrial town before the industrial revolution'[9]. Notable innovations included: the development by William Watts of a new process for making lead shot; the introduction of brass manufacture on a large scale by Abraham Derby (who subsequently moved to Coalbrookdale – the 'cradle of the industrial revolution') and the production by William Cooksworthy of the first English porcelain (the patent was sold to a Staffordshire pottery in 1778 when Cooksworthy was on the verge of Bankruptcy)[10]. In St Phillips there were several iron and lead foundries. One of the foundries even boasted a steam engine used for the boring of cannon.

Among all this innovation and development there was one industry, crucial to the national economy, that was largely missing. In previous centuries Bristol and the surrounding region had been known for its textile industries – in the eighteenth century, the burgeoning cotton industry, one of the great success stories and drivers of Britain's industrial revolution, was noticeable in Bristol by its almost complete absence.

All this manufacturing industry did have its drawbacks in that it polluted the atmosphere and, in some cases, poisoned the soil. While it was generally agreed that in its natural state the Bristol air was remarkably clear, in reality this natural state was a thing of the past. On calm days the air in the Avon valley could be stifling and acrid. 'The smoke issuing from brass-works, glasshouses etc.' observed a trio of visiting artists in 1793, 'keeps the town in almost impenetrable obscurity'[11]. As day trippers from Bath ventured along the Totterdown turnpike their initial impression of Bristol was of a dark satanic landscape of smoking glass houses, iron foundries, distilleries, breweries and sugar houses. When the three artistic gentlemen came to Arnos Vale on the outskirts of Bristol they found 'nothing but smoky brick-kilns and sooty furnaces'[12]. The author, Horace Walpole, was even more damning, describing his first impression of Bristol as being that of 'the dirtiest great shop I ever saw'[13].

Yet this initial impression was misleading. For although Bristol was without the high fashion elegance and sophistication of Bath it did have its own particular charms: Queen Square (the largest square in England after London's Lincoln's Inn) with its mown lawns and gravel walkways; the spectacular and picturesque gorge; even, for the more adventurous, the bustle and cosmopolitan excitement of the quays. All these sights offered the visitor, in the words of

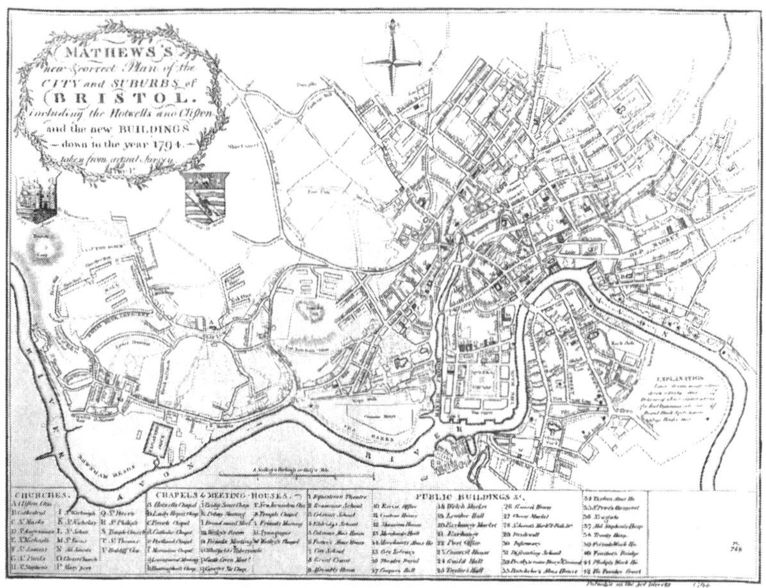

Matthews's map of Bristol, Hotwells and Clifton in 1794. While the ancient city centre retained its old fashioned medieval ambience, the new suburbs of Clifton and the Hotwells offered a more genteel atmosphere.

William Matthews, the possibility of 'ambulatory exercitation'.

While opinions are divided as to the level of cultural stimulation offered by Bristol in the 1790s there can be no doubt that matters had improved since the 1760s[14] when Thomas Chatterton, the boy poet and forger, berated the city for being 'lost to all learning, elegance and sense'. By the end of the century, with its Theatre Royal, its lending library and its Assembly Rooms a variety of entertainments and diversions were on offer. On fashionable occasions at the Theatre Royal, King Street could be crowded with over one hundred private carriages[15]. Bristol was also home to a small group of keen, but uninspiring, writers including Robert Lovell, A.S. & Joseph Cottle, Thomas Beddoes and John Rose[16]. Cottle and Rose – as we shall see later – were also printers and publishers. Entertainment of a less cultural nature was also widely available. Matthews noted that 'The common women are numerous, of all dresses, ranks and prices and nocturnally perambulate as in London'[17] .

Although Bristol could never rival Bath in the pursuit of the arts – nor did it want to – there was one feature of its neighbour that impressed. In the space of 50 years Bath had metamorphosed from a small wool-town to the most elegant city in the Kingdom. Surely Bristol could have a slice of the profitable tourist cake. So, like many other towns during the second half of the eighteenth century, money was soon being spent on developing an up-market and up-wind spa resort. With interest rates stuck at around 4%, building and the purchase of land for building, became a favourite area of speculation.

For a while it looked like the plan to develop Bristol and its environs of Clifton and Hotwells into a fashionable spa might succeed. It is said that there is a wider range and variety of 'Georgian' building in Bristol than in Bath; the majority of it was started (though not always finished) in the 1780s and early 1790s[18]. Yet, while Bath had the classically trained Woods family as architects, the Bristol *nouveau riche* relied largely on the untutored skills of the Paty family. Local stonemasons, the Patys were in demand not just for their Bath-stone ornamentation but also for their clean-cut – if unimaginative – architectural designs. It has to be admitted that Bristol's buildings were of a lesser quality than could be found in its rival along the Avon valley. Contrast, for example, the Royal Crescent in Bath with Royal York Crescent in Clifton. The former is rigidly and brilliantly classical, the latter a delightful shambles. Even so, those viewing the new terraces of Clifton from afar in 1793 were 'struck with agreeable surprise at the sight of a large town hanging in a continued slope, as it were from the very clouds'[19].

For several years the aristocracy and the gentry did indeed come to Bristol, and the neighbouring suburbs of Clifton and Hotwells. The Ostrich Inn (long since demolished, it was at the top end of Whiteladies Road, near the quarry) with its famous bowling green on Durdham Down did a roaring breakfast trade with early morning walkers. Between noon and 2.00 pm the pump room in Hotwells was thronged with visitors taking the soft warm fizzy water that was so good for those who suffered from 'hot acrimonious blood'[20]. In the afternoon the Downs were alive with carriages and equestrians. Or if the tide was right and the weather good there was the opportunity to take a pleasure boat down to 'Ports head' where it was possible to go ashore, and loaded with cold collations 'dine in the woods, which are shady, cool, rural and extremely pleasant'[21].

WAR AND FINANCIAL CRISIS

But as quickly as the popularity of the Hotwells had taken off, it faded. With the outbreak of war with France in February 1793 and the ensuing financial panic many firms were ruined. At one stage, in order to stop a run on the banks, a supply of golden guineas had to be hastily brought from London by stage coach[22]. The Ostrich Inn was empty, the Clifton hotels quiet. The spa's brief heyday was over. Likewise the building boom; the new grand squares and terraces of Clifton – Cornwallis and Royal York Crescents – and elsewhere, were left silent and falling[23]. 'The present war has put a temporary stop', wrote Matthews, 'to these desirable ornaments, real improvements and salutary conveniences'[24]. The financial crisis hit Bristol's builders particularly hard; in April five builders became bankrupt, in May another 15, and by the end of the year it is estimated that one-third of all the builders in the Bristol area were insolvent[25]. The appearance of the suburbs, with their half-completed buildings was reminiscent of a place that had undergone bombardment. Also, the value of property was excessively reduced. Money was not available to complete the new buildings and when sold some produced only a quarter of what had originally been spent on them[26]. The turnabout of Bristol's fortunes in 1793 was rapid. Within two or three months there were nearly 50 considerable local bankruptcies[27]. There was scarcely a tradesman in the city who was not affected in one way or another.

There was also another longer term problem that hung like a dark cloud over Bristol's future. Bristol's lifeblood, the docks, were showing their limitations. The gradual withdrawal from the slave trade and the change in markets brought about by the American Revolution meant a search for new ventures. Yet the possibilities of expansion were limited by the nature of Bristol's port facilities. The topography of the docks had largely been shaped by extensive excavations in the first half of the thirteenth century. Little had been done in the subsequent 500 years or so to upgrade the facilities which, like the roads, were becoming increasingly congested – and in some instances dangerous. Although in their heyday they had been adequate, Bristol's docks, with a 45-foot tidal range six miles up the twisting muddy Avon, were now far from ideal. And because the turn-about for ships using the docks was slow – it could take a total of up six months for the large trans-Atlantic vessels to be checked out by customs, unload their cargo into stores and warehouses, re-stock-up, recruit manpower for the next trip and then prepare for departure – the port was constantly congested. Contemporary pictures of Bristol show a forest of masts above the roof tops; at any time perhaps 200 ships could be berthed along the city's quays. The tides also severely restricted operations – in the year ending March 1793 neap and low tides meant that navigation was impossible on 257 days – in other words for two-thirds of the year the port was inaccessible[28]. The situation was becoming intolerable; Bristol's merchants were concerned, and had been for many years, that the competitive edge of the port was declining.

The proposed remedy, first put forward in 1720, was a floating harbour that would overcome the difficulties of operating round the tides. Such a radical, but necessary, cure to the docks' problems would require clear and focused backing from the Corporation and the overseers of Bristol's docks, the Merchant Venturers. It would be ten years, however, before such a scheme was officially authorised, and an additional six years before it was fully completed[29].

So, in his Bristol guide Matthews had presented a view of Bristol as residents would have liked the city to be seen, rather than how it actually was. The picture, as with most tourist brochures, was distorted. For 500 years Bristol's position after London had been supreme. But the rapid growth in the eighteenth century of Birmingham, Leeds, Manchester, Newcastle and several other cities had put an end to this proud boast. To anyone who had recently travelled to Liverpool and the North East of England the claim that Bristol was still the country's second city was a preposterous conceit. Although Bristol was certainly not in overall decline, indeed the city was proud of the absence of beggars on its streets, its rate of expansion was nothing like as rapid as the new industrial cities of the North. In other words, Bristol had lost its cherished second city status. King cotton had toppled Bristol from its provincial throne.

Notes

1. Matthews, p.2.
2. Minchinton, W,. The Port of Bristol in the Eighteenth Century, ed. Mc Grath, P., (1972), p.131. 3. MacInnes, C.M., Bristol and the Slave Trade in Bristol in the eighteenth century, ed. McGrath P., (1972) p. 162.
4. MacInnes, C.M., Bristol and the Slave Trade in Bristol in the Eighteenth Century, ed. McGrath P., (1972) p. 168.
5. Minchinton, W., The Port of Bristol in the Eighteenth Century ed. Mc Grath, P., (1972), p.131.
6. Pinney Papers, Business Letter-book, 1805–7, fol.273. Quoted in Macinnes, C.M., Bristol: A Gateway of Empire.
7. Matthews, p. 38.
8. Matthews, p. 44–45.
9. Little, B., The City and County of Bristol, (1954), p. 154.
10. Witt, C., Bristol Fine Wares 1670-1970, (1980) p.7.
11. Messrs. Ibbetson, Laporte and Hassell, A Picturesque Guide to Bath, Bristol Hot-Wells, the River Avon and Adjacent Country (1793), p.155.
12. Ibid p.153.
13. Marcy, P.T., Eighteenth Century Views of Bristol and Bristolians in Bristol in the eighteenth century, ed. Mc Grath, P., (1972) p. 20.
14. James, R.I., Bristol Society in the Eighteenth Century in MacInnes, C.M. & Whittard, W.F. Bristol & Its Adjoining Counties (1955), p. 231–41. Holmes, R. Coleridge: Early Visions (1990), p. 92.
15. James, R.I. p. 240.
16. Lamoine, G. Notes on Bristol's Literary Circle (Toulouse 1973) B.R.L. B.26474
17. Matthews p. 90.
18. Mowl, T., To Build the Second City (1991) p. 9.
19. Matthews p. 2.
20. Matthews p. 101.
21. Matthews p. 104.
22. Mr Seyer's Manuscripts relating to the History of Bristol, B.R.L. B.4533, p. 39.
23. Latimer p. 495.
24. Matthews p. 42.
25. Jones, D., A History of Clifton (1992) p. 78.
26. Mr Seyer's Manuscripts, p. 39.
27. Latimer p. 500.
28. Lord J. & Southam J., The Floating Harbour (1983) p. 34.
29. Lord J. & Southam J., p. 36–7.

THREE

Late September 1793

So, what was going on in Bristol during the autumn of 1793? The following items of news are extracted from the Bristol Gazette and Public Advertiser for 26 September of that year.

Britain had now been at war for just over seven months. One only had to walk along the quays of Bristol to see the effect of the hostilities. Perhaps the most obvious difference was that more ships were openly armed than in previous times. Thus when touting for trade and passengers The Jonah, crewed by 30 men and shortly leaving for Cork, Antigua and Montserrat, made special mention that it was equipped with ten guns. On the other hand, the Brigantine Catherine announced that it was determined to sail to the West Indies in one month 'with or without convoy'. The news from abroad was good. With Admiral Hood's capture of the harbour of Toulon there was a feeling of optimism in the air.

Nearer to home, despite spiralling inflation and the uncertain state of the local economy, a couple of major civil engineering ventures were being planned. Canal schemes were all the vogue and designs for the Kennet and Avon Canal were well underway. A meeting for another venture, the ill-fated Bristol and Western Canal, which was projected to run from Bristol to Exeter via Taunton, was held on the 24 September.

Yet if the business people of Bristol wanted to support a really worthwhile local venture they needed to look no further than their own docks. On 26 September it was announced that, at long last, moves were to be made to address the problems of the port by presenting an application for improvements to the next session of Parliament[1].

Celebrations were also in order for the opening of the Bristol Brewery's new brewhouse in Bath Street (later to become part of the site of Courage's Brewery). Finest old porter was offered for sale in casks or bottles.

Domestic builders were, however, facing hard times during the autumn of 1793. The state of the domestic housing market, echoing that of the economy generally, was not good. As has been mentioned earlier, speculation on house building had come to an abrupt end. One casualty of the house building slump during the last week of September 1793 was timber merchant and builder James Lockier. A victim of the recent rise in interest rates, Lockier, now bankrupt, was forced to sell his remaining four houses in Richmond Terrace at a knock-down price.

On the other hand, for the more leisured classes there were a number of events to look forward to. Rehearsals were underway at the Theatre Royal in King Street for the next production, a double bill, which included a comedy 'The Natural Son' and the 'Highland Reel', a musical entertainment in three acts. The dwindling social scene in Hotwells, meanwhile, had been temporarily enhanced by the arrival of Sir Henry and Lady Beauchamp Proctor. Preparations were in hand for a charity ball for 'three women in great distress' soon to be held at the Hotwells.

In the surrounding countryside the current rise of prices was making the temptation of a free meal from a stray pheasant or hare increasingly irresistible. But the game laws were strict – an act of 1770 threatened a year's imprisonment for those who took game at night. And even when a tasty morsel strayed into a backyard the law laid down that it was illegal to kill it. Only landed gentlemen had that prerogative[2]. Even so, game was becoming scarce to the south of Bristol and in the Pensford, Compton Dando and Stanton Drew area landowners had joined together for the prosecution and punishment of poachers. The association offered a reward of two guineas for information leading to a successful indictment.

For those caught committing petty crime the punishments could be severe. At the Bristol September quarter sessions the Bristol Gazette and Public Advertiser reported that a Mr T. Gregory was punished for taking butter from his master by transportation for seven years. With a six penny fine and a three month jail sentence Anne Lewis was treated more leniently for her crime of stealing blankets and sheets. Life in Bristol's Newgate gaol – the whitewashed building was described by the prison reformer John Howard as 'white without and foul within' – was no easy option[3]. To supplement their meagre rations the prisoners were allowed to hang a collecting box outside the main gate. Over the previous three months 'the humane and generous public' had deposited £1 2s. 6d.

For anyone who did have few pennies to spare there was the opportunity to dream of untold riches. Tickets for both the Irish and English state lotteries were on sale for sixpence. (Lotteries were used to finance the building of Westminster Bridge and the British Museum. They were ended by Parliament in 1826.) The draw for the English lottery was to be held on 17 February 1794; at the previous lottery the top prize had been a phenomenal £30,000.

Finally, on 21 September 1793 the lease for the Bristol Bridge Toll, the lease that most people had expected to come to an end, was auctioned at the Exchange Coffee House in Corn Street. In itself the auction was nothing out of the ordinary. Yet the sale was to set in motion a series of events that were to rank as one of the bloodiest and most shameful incidents in Bristol's long history. Even so, as September 1793 drew to a close, there was little to forewarn that the month would end so dramatically[4].

'TOLLS TO LET'

Notice of the auction appeared on Saturday 7 September 1793 in Felix Farley's Bristol Journal:

To Let by Auction
At the Exchange Coffee House
on Saturday the 21st September
The Tolls payable for passing over Bristol Bridge
together with the two toll houses.

Further details: Mr Thomas Symons – Attorney at Law
Thomas Booth, Broker

No one was more alarmed by the news of the forthcoming sale than the present leasee of the tolls, Mr Abraham Hiscoxe. For when Hiscoxe had taken over the lease for £2,150 at the previous Michelmas, it was generally understood that this would be the toll's last year. This expectation had been confirmed independently by both Wintour Harris, Deputy Chamberlain to the Bristol Corporation and Thomas Symonds, the lawyer who oversaw the letting of the bridge. Wintour Harris had said that the Bridge Committee already had £3,000 in hand and would be able to discharge every debt while still having a surplus to fund future repairs of the bridge[5].

However, unknown to Hiscoxe, sometime during the previous

months, the Bridge Commissioners had adjusted their calculations and found that the figures did not balance as well as they had thought. This was not the first time that the Bridge Commissioners had got their sums wrong. For many years there had been a general suspicion that the bridge's finances had been handled carelessly – even dishonestly. Matters were not helped, indeed distrust was increased, by the Commissioner's refusal to produce their accounts. Eventually a public enquiry in 1789 forced the Commissioners to publish their accounts annually. Even then the detail contained in the balance sheet was so limited that it rendered it virtually meaningless. Nevertheless, calculating from these statements, many people had assumed that the toll would cease at the end of Bristol's administrative year, on the 29 September 1793[6].

However, by their latest reckoning the Bridge Commissioners only had £2,000 in hand, a sum that was deemed insufficient to generate enough interest to pay for the lighting and ongoing repairs. Therefore, in order to save the citizens of Bristol the effort and expense of another application to Parliament to authorise the raising of further funds, it was decided that it would be far more straightforward to simply extend the lease for another year[7]. This was a decision that seriously underestimated the strength of feeling against the tolls and, indeed, all that they stood for.

THE BRISTOL CORPORATION – 'A SELF-EXISTING EVIL'

Bristol was unusual in that by its Charter of 1373 it was both a city and county in its own right. This meant that it had its own courts and its own sheriff. The Council of Bristol consisted of a Mayor, a Recorder, twelve Aldermen (each of whom presided

Bristol's docks were becoming increasingly congested. With a 45 ft tidal range six miles up the twisting Avon, they were far from ideal. The proposed remedy – a floating harbour – had first been suggested in 1720. (City of Bristol Museum and Art Gallery)

over one of the city wards), two sheriffs, an under-sheriff and 28 common-councilmen. There was also a town clerk, who had to be a barrister of at least three years standing, who presided as a judge at the quarter sessions. Yet, despite its outward impression of grandeur, by the late eighteenth century, the Council generated little respect from the general populace of Bristol. It was felt that members of the Council were out of touch with the realities of the time. Rather than concentrating on matters of major significance for the city, the Council was more interested in spending its money on expensive self-aggrandising ceremonies. The Mayor was rarely seen in the streets as he would travel only by carriage; while the acquisition in 1781 of the Mansion House in Queen Square and the subsequent refurbishment with chandeliers and luxurious carpets had been viewed by many as an unnecessary extravagance[8]. The

Council's hospitality was legendary; at the slightest excuse a barrel of Bristol Milk or wine would be tapped. As the city entered a new era, the Council clung to its old pretensions – sometimes to ridiculous lengths. In 1792 Mayor John Noble, a tall and imposing figure, clad in his mayoral scarlet robes edged with ermine, entered the Old Bailey in London and, with all the pomp he could muster, took his place on the judge's bench. When questioned about his presence, to the disbelief of the other judges, he produced an ancient charter containing a long forgotten clause asserting that Mayors of Bristol were constituted as judges of the Old Bailey. And then, having made his point, John Noble left. On his return to Bristol the Common Council gave a vote of thanks to the Mayor for his fine performance[9]. At times it seemed as if Bristol's ruling elite had lost touch with the real world.

At the heart of the problem was the fact that Bristol's Council was self-electing. Thanks to an updated charter granted by Queen Anne in 1710 Council Officers were self-appointed; and not only that – they were also granted their posts for life. Thus, there was no public voting; aldermen and councillors were elected for life by fellow councillors, whilst the mayor usually chose his own successor. With no democratic process there was little opportunity for new blood, new energy or new ideas to permeate through the city's government.

Unlike many other cities of the time, where the aristocracy exerted powerful influences, Bristol was ruled by an elite of merchant traders. One only has to look at the list of Corporation members for 1793 to see that the same merchant families – the Ames, the Bengoughs, the Daubenys, the Eltons, the Harfords and so on – had been represented for several previous generations. (Perhaps even more alarming was the shadowy role played by the Society of the Merchant Venturers. The Society of Merchant Venturers, established way back in 1552, represented the merchants of the city and exercised control over the river and the port. It has often been said that this secretive freemasonry was the real power behind the throne. To muddy matters even more membership of the Merchant Venturers and the Corporation was largely interchangeable.) Of course, Bristol's local government was not untypical. Over the next forty years there was an increasing national demand for reform. Locally this eventually led to the Bristol Reform riots of 1831 – but that is another story.

This is not to say that Bristol's ruling class was always one big happy family. Arguments between competitors in trade, and personal rivalries, could spill out into the public arena. In 1786, Sam 'Devil' Worral used such disrespectful language to fellow councillor George Daubeny that he was dismissed from his post as clerk to the Merchant Venturers[10].

Although the self-electing nature of the Corporation had its problems, matters were made worse by its attitude to public affairs. A frequent criticism of the Corporation was that although it wanted power, it was unwilling to accept responsibility[11].

One of the Corporation's most outspoken critics was the printer, bookseller and literary dabbler John Rose. In 1792 Rose wrote and published a pamphlet – clearly influenced by the writings of Thomas Paine – entitled 'Free Thoughts on the Offices of Mayor Alderman and Common Council of the City of Bristol'[12]. Rose compared the government of Bristol with that of London where members of the Common Council were elected annually by the inhabitants of wards rather than for life by fellow common councillors. When it came to financial accountability Rose claimed that in London 'receipts and disbursements (are) published annually; in Bristol no accounts (are) published'[13] . 'The offices of Mayor, Alderman and Common

Council of the City of Bristol, are what ought not to exist in this country", Rose continued. 'They are', he concluded, 'a local tyranny; a partial oppression; an arbitrary government within a limited one; a self creative, self existing-evil...'[14]. In short, Rose recommended the 'annihilation' of the Bristol Corporation.

This was strong stuff, for when Rose attacked the City's ruling elite he was also setting himself up in the public mind as a republican – an especially dangerous stance to take once the country was at war with France. John Rose's views would have been unpopular with the ruling classes at anytime; in 1792 they were seen as particularly invidious.

'A TOLL-KEEPER'S LOT IS NOT A HAPPY ONE'

On Thursday evening the present renters of the Bristol Bridge Toll, notwithstanding the year for which they took them will not expire before the 29th instant, discontinued collecting the same, and having taken away the gate, opened a free passage for carriages, horses etc which have since continued to go over toll free. On the occasion a large concourse of people assembled on the bridge, and testified their approbation by means of a bonfire, firing guns and squibs, and other marks of joy and exultation: – But as the tolls are advertised to be let this day, for another year, it remains to be seen whether the collection of them is to be resumed.

Felix Farley's Bristol Journal
Saturday, 21 September 1793

Despite his conversation earlier in the year, Thomas Symons later asked Abraham Hiscoxe whether he would be interested in taking on the tolls again. Hiscoxe could see a potential storm brewing – a storm that, if he was not very careful, would be heading right his way. Hiscoxe knew that an extension to the toll would be unpopular and would provoke resentment, even violence – some of which would undoubtedly be directed at himself and his team of toll-collectors; at the best of times a toll-keeper's lot was not a happy one. Fearing the likely violent consequences of renewing his lease, Hiscoxe, without the slightest hesitation, replied to Symons that he would have nothing to do with it[15].

Indeed, Hiscoxe was so concerned about the impending danger that he resolved to take action. It had once been said – exactly by whom nobody could say – that if the collection of the toll was to lapse for ten days a new Act of Parliament was required to reinstate it. Hiscoxe therefore decided to abandon the collection of the toll on the morning of Friday 20 September. Although he would lose his income for that period, he intended to try to recoup his loses by asking for contributions from his more loyal 'customers'. More importantly he would escape the likelihood of further insults, threats and actual violence[16].

News of Hiscoxe's plan must have spread, for on the night before he had intended to relinquish the charge a man drove to the bridge and insisted on crossing free of charge. A quarrel ensued between the collector of the toll for that evening, William Collins, and the carter who eventually got his own way[17]. Once one person had gone for free the floodgates burst. Finding it impossible to continue the collection, the gates were opened and unpaid passage was allowed. The news spread quickly. A crowd gathered, a couple of barrels of beer appeared as if from nowhere, and soon celebrations were in full swing. Spectators lined the bridge and cheered as, for the first time in 25 years, horses and carriages crossed the bridge without charge. In good natured, rumbustious fun the boards advertising the charges, together with the redundant toll gates, were thrown, in the time-honoured tradition of turnpike demonstrations, onto a bonfire[18]. What was surprising was that nobody intervened - no magistrates, constables or watchmen appeared on the scene to restore law and order. With hindsight many people were to suggest that had the authorities taken a firm stance then, the city would have been spared all the trouble that was to follow. Even so, on that Thursday evening, at long last, Bristol's citizens had reclaimed their rights to the city's most important highway.

The euphoria of Thursday evening was, as the report in Felix Farley's Bristol Journal intimated, short-lived. The Bridge Trustees were not to be dissuaded. The next day, Friday, the Trustees offered a reward of 50 guineas for discovery of the identity of the offenders who had burnt the gates and the toll board. Even more alarming was the trustees affirmation that the Bristol Bridge Act of 1756 stood, as did the punishment for taking down the toll board - death. They also stated - and this was hardest of all to believe - that a debt of £2,500 remained[19].

The Saturday auction for the lease of the tolls for one more year went ahead as advertised. In the previous year the lease had sold for £2,150. But this time, reflecting the precarious situation, the bidding was not high. Eventually, in a partnership that was verging on the improper, Wintour Harris, Deputy Chamberlain to the Corporation and the attorney Thomas Symons, secured the lease for the knockdown sum of £1,920[20]. Resumption of the collection of the toll was scheduled to start again on Sunday 29 September. It seemed as if Hiscoxe's bold plan was not going to work after all.

'THE RIGHTS OF MAN'

A new loyal song for the 1st January 1793;
the 104th year of Britain's Liberty

God save great George our King
Long live our noble King,
God save the King!

Let the reformer Paine
Know his vile arts are vain;
Britain is free!

Confound his politicks,
Frustrate his knavish tricks
With Equal laws we mix
True liberty.

England staunch soldiery
Proof against treachery
Bravely unite, ...

Felix Farley's Bristol Journal
Saturday, 19 January 1793

Bristolians were, of course, well aware of the revolutionary events occurring in France and elsewhere across Europe at this time. Not only were they kept up-to-date by the informal communications network of a cosmopolitan port, they were also extremely well served by newspapers. In 1793 the City had five weekly newspapers – more than any other provincial town in the country[21]. As Bristolians drank their morning coffee they were able to read about the latest events in France. Although war with France during the eighteenth century was commonplace, the French Revolutionary war was worryingly different in that it posed additional threats to the British Constitution. While in 1789 reactions to the storming of the Bastille and the challenge to the despotism of the *Ancien Regime* had been largely favourable, by 1793, as anarchy and atheism appeared to take a grip in France, alarm slowly began to spread. The French Revolution, now in its fourth year, was taking an increasingly brutal and irrational hold; Dr Guillotin's new instrument of execution was to be seen in regular service in Paris' *Place de la Revolution*. While the French Revolution was initially perceived as a process mirroring Britain's Glorious Revolution of 1688, subsequent events were now proving that the changes were an altogether stronger cup of tea than those brewed in England one hundred years before.

Edmund Burke, a Member of Parliament for Bristol between 1774 and 1780, had foreseen trouble right from the beginning. He warned his fellow MPs as early as 1790 that if this revolutionary zeal was to spread that they would have:

their mansions pulled down and pillaged, their persons abused, insulted, and destroyed, their title-deeds brought out and burned before their faces...[22]

Three years later Burke's prophecies seemed to be frighteningly accurate. On Saturday 26 January 1793 Bristolians opened their *Felix Farley's Bristol Journal* to read:

Murder of Louis XVI
Paris, Monday January 21
Twelve o'clock at noon

The unfortunate Louis is no
more. He was beheaded at ten
o'clock in Place de Louis Quinze

With the astounding news of Louis XVI's execution the not so distant thunder across the Channel was a sobering reminder of what could happen in England if the likes of the French had their way.

In spite of Louis's execution the French revolutionaries still had a few British supporters – the chief of whom was Thomas Paine. Thomas Paine and revolution seemed to go hand in hand. In 1776 Paine's pamphlet 'Common Sense' caught the American imagination and provided inspiration for the leaders of the American War of Independence. Thirteen years later, when Paine was visiting France on a bridge building project, he was able to offer the leaders of the revolution the benefit of his expertise. (It should be pointed out that Paine was a brave opponent of the execution of Louis XVI, as the French King had been an ally to the Americans during their own revolution.)

When Paine's 'The Rights of Man', written in response to Burke's attack on the French, was published in 1792 those in authority became seriously concerned[23]. In his typically egalitarian style Paine promoted a number of ideas, some of which we take for granted today. In the eighteenth century, however, they were truly extraordinary. Paine believed: that all men are equal; that the monarchy and the aristocracy should be abolished; that the poor should be provided with relief; that education should be available for all and that the elderly should be allocated an annual pension[24]. 'When we see', Paine wrote with simple eloquence, 'age going to the workhouse and youth going to the gallows something must be wrong in the system of government'[25].

Like Bristol's John Rose, Paine also directed his venom at self-electing Corporations. 'It is a perversion of terms to say that a charter gives rights', wrote Paine, 'it operates to the contrary effect, that of taking rights away'[26]. The 'Rights of Man' attracted unprecedented interest with an estimated readership of more than 200,000 people[27]. The Prime Minister, William Pitt the Younger, was particularly unimpressed by Paine's home-grown radicalism and took steps to silence him. In December 1792, while Paine was abroad in France, he was found guilty in his absence of seditious libel and was subsequently unable to ever return to his native country. In Bristol, Paine wielded a double edged sword. Not only was he thought to be stirring seditious ideas against the system of local government, but he was also an ardent campaigner against slavery. Certainly, whatever the viewpoint Paine had undeniably captured the public mind.

Yet Bristol had never been a hotbed of radicalism, even during the later part of the eighteenth century. In reality the radical views of John Rose would have elicited little popular support. At public meetings of every kind, the contemporary historian Samuel Seyer reported that 'God Save the King' was 'sung with most violent enthusiasm'. And at the beginning of 1793 the Common Council took the unusual step of promoting its patriotism by publishing a resolution in favour of the constitution[28]. Hardly a week went by without the local newspapers denouncing Paine and the spectre of republicanism. On the 17 December 1792, in the ever-popular and time-honoured way, an effigy of Paine was burnt in public. In fact the burning was so successful that a similar therapeutic protest was carried out the following night. And again on February 26 1793[29].

Not surprisingly, all French nationals resident in Britain – even those who had fled the revolution – were viewed with suspicion. The Mayor of Liverpool informed his counterpart in Bristol, Henry Bengough, on 13 January 1793 that he had received an anonymous letter, postmarked Bath (where there were a number of French residents), which contained threats of sabotage to the Liverpool docks[30]. In his letter of reply Bengough confirmed that he had consequently warned Bristol's dock watch 'to be vigilant against designs so exceedingly mischievous and diabolical'[31].

With the outbreak of war in February 1793 paranoia set-in in earnest. Echoing Burke's alarm, an anonymous correspondent wrote to *Felix Farely's Bristol Journal* with the following warning:

The Rights of Man
Addressed to Englishmen

...let the situation in France be a warning to you. Has the right of personal security been respected there? Their own convention confessed that several hundred of innocent citizens were dragged last September from the prisons and barbarously murdered. Has the right of personal liberty been preserved...when those miserable victims were without any form of accusation, loaded into fetters and plunged into dungeons Has the right of personal property been maintained? That question I believe will need no reply. You know, you feel what are the RIGHTS OF MAN in England. What are the rights of man in France, except those of plundering and slaughtering, I am unable to tell you.

An Englishman[32]

With the country at war and revolution sweeping across Europe support of the status quo was of paramount importance. Thus another correspondent to *Felix Farley's Bristol Journal* was even more prophetic when he pleaded for support of the city's magistrates during such difficult times:

Mr Printer,

I have no doubt but the resolution of our worthy Magistrates and inhabitants of this city, will meet with the approbation and consent of every well wisher to our most excellent constitution. The more unanimity we discover in the prosecution of those resolutions, the more we shall certainly lessen the danger we may face from the machinations and plots of evil and designing men.'[33]

The authorities were nervous. By September, despite little real local supporting evidence, there was a fear of spies, *agent provocateurs* and revolution in the autumn air.

Notes

1. The plans were subsequently put on hold due to the war.
2. Gilmour, I., Riots, Risings and Revolution (1992), p.142.
3. Latimer p.407
4. All the events quoted in this section have been extracted from The Bristol Gazette and Public Advertiser for 26 September 1793.
5. Committee, p.20.
6. Mr Seyer's Manuscripts relating to the History of Bristol, BRL B.4533 p.41.
7. Bristol Gazette and Public Advertiser, 3 October 1793.
8. Latimer p.450.
9. Latimer p.495.
10. Way, L.J., An Account of Leigh Woods (Bristol & Gloucestershire Archaeological Society, Vol 36, 1913) p. 88.
11. Ralph, E., Government of Bristol (1973) p.25.
12. Rose, J., Free Thoughts on the Offices of Mayor, Alderman and Common Council of the City of Bristol (1792), B.R.L. B.25365.

Satirical engraving celebrating George Daubeny's 1781 election victory with a 'glorious majority of 372'. A slave stands behind liberty. Outraged by Daubeny's 'many acts of bribery and corruption' over 1,000 citizens put their name on a petition protesting against his election. (City of Bristol Museum and Art Gallery)

13. Ibid p.10.
14. Ibid p.9.
15. Committee, p.7.
16. Committee, p.21.
17. Committee, p.21.
18. Committee, p.8.
19. Rose, p.6.
20. Committee, p.14.
21. The Bristol Mercury was published on Mondays; the Bristol Gazette on Wednesday evenings; Sarah Farley's Journal, Bonner and Middleton's Journal and Felix Farley's Bristol Journal were all published on Saturdays. Anon., Early Bristol Newspapers (1956).
22. Colley, L., Britons (1994) p.150.
23. Paine did little to promote female rights; this was left to Mary Wollstonecraft with the publication of "A Vindication of the Rights of Women", (1794).
24. Foot, M. & Kramnick, I.(eds), Thomas Paine Reader (1987) pp.20-1.
25. Foot, M. & Kramnick,I.(eds), Thomas Paine Reader (London 1987) p.314.
26. ibid. p.317.
27. Thompson, E.P., The Making of the English Working Class (1968) p.117.
28. B.R.O. Town Clerk's box 1793.
29. Mr Seyer's Manuscripts, p.l7.
30. B.R.O. Town Clerk's Correspondence Box 1792, bundle 13.
31. B.R.O. Town Clerk's Correspondence Book, 16 Jan. 1793.
32. F.F.J., 16 February 1793.
33. F.F.J., 12 January 1793.

FOUR

'Saturday nights... are the best adapted for a riot'

Ever since the evening of Thursday 19 September no charge had been levied for crossing Bristol Bridge. Nine days later, on the morning of Saturday 28 September workmen appeared and erected new gates in preparation for the re-introduction of the toll the next day. This was not good timing. If there was going to be trouble it would be on a Saturday night when the week's wages were spent on ale and heads lightened by alcohol. In Bristol rational thinking was certainly not part of the Saturday night tradition. As one commentator wrote after the event: it is 'an established fact...that Saturday nights, of all others, are the best adapted for a riot'[1].

As had happened only nine days before, a crowd gathered in the evening, faggots were taken from the Back, and soon the new gates were part of a roaring bonfire. The first Magistrate to appear on the scene was George Daubeny. An energetic and wiry 51-year-old, Daubeny was a stalwart of the Corporation and a prime example of Bristol's exclusive ruling elite. He had joined the Common Council in 1767 at the age of 25, and between 1781 and 1784 he was one of Bristol's two Members of Parliament[2]. As part of his parliamentary election campaign Daubeny had provided patriotic free dinners at the *Full Moon* in Stokes Croft where those eligible to vote were invited to try 'the difference between American bull beef and the roast beef of Old England'[3]. (This was a reference to Daubeny's rival Henry Cruger, an American.) Not everyone was so easily influenced, however. Indeed over 1,000 citizens, outraged by Daubeny's 'many acts of bribery and corruption and other partial and illegal practices and proceedings', put their names on a petition to the House of Commons protesting Daubeny's election[4]. During the following election in 1784 Daubeny narrowly missed re-election by just 70 votes. The Daubeny family initially made their money through sugar refining though later expanded to a number of other commercial ventures such as the Ames, Cave, Harford and Daubeny Bank in Corn Street. There were four consecutive generations of George Daubeny[5]. This George, who was generation number three, was the most outwardly successful – and ruthless – of the family. Although a man of undoubted ability there was a less attractive side to his character. At times 'George the Vain'[6], as he was sometimes called, would behave like a bully with a short fuse. He also had a reputation for backing up his arguments with verbal and even physical intimidation. On this occasion, true to character, Daubeny openly vented his anger, swearing and lashing out at the crowd. When he attempted to collar a bystander a scuffle broke out and Daubeny was knocked to the ground. A dangerous pattern was beginning to develop. It was obviously beyond the power of just one magistrate, even George Daubeny, to contain the situation. Something had to be done before matters got seriously out of hand.

BRISTOL'S VIOLENT CENTURY

In reality the disturbance that Daubeny confronted was not out of the ordinary. As Matthews wrote of his fellow Bristolians: 'The populace are apt to collect in mobs on the slightest occasions'[7]. Throughout the eighteenth century Bristol's everyday life was interrupted by civil disturbances. In this Bristol was not unique – indeed several historians have categorised the eighteenth century as being the century of the riot.

Of course, the eighteenth century was a time of great economic and social transformation. As the country moved from an agrarian to an industrial economy the very fabric of English society changed at unprecedented rate. For the urban labouring classes, faced with longer working hours and sometimes horrendous new industrial workplaces, these were frequently changes for the worse. Protests were often a result of change rather than a desire for change. As E.P.Thompson has pointed out it was often the case that the people felt they had to defend their traditional 'constitution' against the forces of 'progress'[8].

Paradoxically, during the eighteenth century the British were proud to boast about their inalienable right to freedom. This sacred freedom had been bestowed through the Glorious Revolution of 1688 – the country had been through its own process of radical change nearly one hundred years before the French embarked on their tortuous journey of liberation.

Yet, in practice, for the common working person, this particularly British concept of freedom – liberty without equality – amounted to very little. In fact, with no political rights and little means of exerting any political pressure, about the only way for the propertyless majority to address any grievance was to resort to the power of the crowd.

During the first half of the century hardly a decade went by in Bristol without some sort of major commotion. There were food riots in 1709, 1753 and 1756, riots against dissenters in 1714, against Jews in 1753 and Turnpike riots in 1727 and 1749[9]. (There is a tale, probably apocryphal, that during protests against wage cuts in 1754

Bristolians are reputed to have demonstrated an early example of national stereotyping by chanting 'No French...No...Garlic!'[10].) There were also times when the people's moral sensibilities were so outraged that they took the law into their own hands. For instance, on 5 November 1792 (5 November was always a good night for impromptu revenge) two women who had committed some unspecified crimes (they were probably running brothels) had their homes torn down and reduced to rubble by a mob of over 100 people[11].

Demonstrations were often largely concerned with local fears and the minutiae of everyday life rather than the wider issues of social or political change. Certainly, for anyone in the West Country who harboured revolutionary ideas a half-remembered folk memory held sway over the people's minds. The ferocity of Judge Jeffreys' bloody assize of 1685 was effective in making many generations of potential rebels think twice. 'Popular rebellion' wrote the social historian George Rudé, 'had lost its sharp edge since Monmouth's defeat at Sedgemore'[12].

It should be pointed out that although the ruling elite was against violence in principle, they were not always above manipulating the crowd for their own means. For instance, violence organised from 'above' was a common feature of election campaigns in Bristol. Of course, the election process was very different from today, in that voting was done publically and the polls could stay open for as long as forty days. Voters – and candidates – were frequently subjected to verbal and physical intimidation by hired mobs that had been excited by copious amounts of free alcohol. During the 1766 election campaign it is estimated that 48 inns within the city were opened for free 'general entertainment'[13]. Although this hospitality did at least give the non-voters a feeling that they were participating in the electoral process, there were obvious dangers in such forms of bribery; the enthusiasms of a drunken mob are, of course, difficult to contain and are likely to stray in unexpected directions. In the 1781 election campaign between George Daubeny and Henry Cruger, a drunken mob of Cruger supporters took an indiscriminate dislike to some Welsh sailors from Swansea and in the ensuing battle two men were killed and a number injured, including several children[14].

In short, the threat – real or imaginary – of the mob formed a constant backdrop to Bristol's political arena. Indeed the spectre of the untamed, unwashed and heathen Kingswood miners marauding through the city acted as a frequent brake to the excesses of the Corporation. By the middle of the century, despite one historian's observation that 'riot is rarely the effect of wont but rather the spirit of wantonness'[15] the Corporation was so aware of the potential for public disorder caused by the fluctuation of food prices that they made special arrangements to keep the larder stocked. (Apart from in 1709, 1726–8 and 1740 when the harvests failed, the problem was with the local distribution of food, rather than a nationwide dearth.) Thus in 1766, at a time of sharp price increases, when many neighbouring towns – Stroud, Tetbury, Bath and Gloucester – were rocked by violence[16], calm was maintained in Bristol through a substantial subsidy of corn prices by the Corporation[17].

LAW ENFORCEMENT

Although Bristol was no stranger to civil disturbance the science of crowd control was nevertheless still in its infancy. In fact, in the absence of any effective police force the options for the control of law and order were extremely limited. While, in theory, every ward had a chief constable, a night constable and several 'charlies' (night-watchmen) stationed in sentry boxes, the very act of them all responding to a summons was an achievement in itself. On this particular Saturday night the turnout was particularly poor. Consequently, with such a depleted force the parish constables were powerless, and far too concerned for their own safety, to mount any effective control[18]. The only alternative, and this was an extreme alternative, was to call out the militia.

Raised by conscription, the militia was the Kingdom's standing army. Any healthy male between the age of 18 and 50 could be selected by ballot to serve for three years. Although overseas service was expressly ruled out, few conscripts doubted that if the worst came to the worst they could be shipped abroad. The implementation of the 1757 Militia Acts was so unpopular it had provoked widespread rioting. There was, however, an opt-out clause – the payment of a £10 fine; the equivalent of roughly six months wages for a labourer. Needless to say it was a fee that few of the labouring poor had to hand or were able to raise[19].

Although being called up for the militia was undoubtedly a constant fear, in Bristol it was the press gang who were held in even greater dread. The press gang's feared regime was all too well known to the young men of Bristol. Although Bristol was not a major naval port, during wartime in particular, the city's inns were liable to raids and merchant seamen forcibly enlisted. Another ploy of the press gang was to approach ships nearing their home port. In 1756 the Bristol ship the *Virginia Merchant*, which was returning from the West Indies, was boarded by a press gang in the Bristol Channel. The crew put up such fierce resistance that the commander of the 'recruiting' vessel opened fire. The *Virginia Merchant* was so badly damaged that it sank[20]. In March 1793, given the current emergency,

Henry Bengough, Mayor of Bristol from 1792–93. His last day in office must have been a time he would have liked to forget. (Effigy: Lord Mayor's Chapel)

the Mayor of Bristol received an order from London to 'impress as many seamen and seafaring men, of strong bodies and good health, as you possibly can procure'. By the end of the year the Mayor was able to report that the astounding number of 452 men had been enlisted[21]. How many of these went of their own free will was not recorded.

The authorities were wary about the use of the militia in civil disturbances; indeed, there was a nagging doubt that the soldiers might even sympathise with the aims and actions of those they were called out to quell. For this reason the militia were strictly subject to the common law of the land, to such an extent that their situation could sometimes become untenable. If the soldiers fired on a crowd they could be tried for murder; if they refused they could be executed for mutiny. To make matters even more complicated, and cause potential confusion in the chain of command, the militia were under the orders, not of their own officers, but of the local magistrates. If things went wrong it was the magistrates who had to shoulder the blame.

The standard procedure for calling out the troops was so long-winded that help often arrived well after the crisis had passed – no bad thing perhaps, for records invariably indicate that the worst physical violence was inflicted by the authorities on the crowd, rather than the other way round. In theory, a request for help was to be sent to the Secretary of State in London and, if approved, passed on to the War Office. The Secretary at War would then issue an order to the nearest body of troops. On this occasion, realising that this rigmarole would take a couple of days, Mayor Bengough by-passed the official routes and sought reinforcements directly. This was not a particularly wise course of action; if the situation got out of control there could be repercussions. Admittedly, Mayor Bengough was under pressure and there were troops close at hand; nevertheless in the course of time such a decision would prove to be both reckless and naive. Indeed Bengough could be putting his own neck at risk. It was not without precedent for a mayor to be tried for murder after the quelling of a riot had gone seriously wrong – for them to be actually found guilty was another matter!

On this autumn night in 1793 it was the Hereford Militia, in Bristol to look after the French prisoners at the Stapleton Road goal, who had the misfortune to be summoned to the affray on the bridge.

'REMEMBER, THEY FIRED WITHOUT MY ORDERS OR CONSENT.'

By the time the militia reached the city centre the bonfire was merely a low pile of glowing embers and the people were drifting away. As the sound of the fife and drum drew nearer those responsible for the fire melted into the remaining crowd. Yet the sight of the magistrates and their armed entourage had exactly the opposite effect of what had been intended. As the militia marched through the streets of the city many were drawn by curiosity to follow them. The earlier excitement was rekindled, spectators drifted back and soon the crowd was bigger than it had been in the first place[22].

Unfortunately, the very act of summoning the militia ushered in a new dimension to the protests. The essence of successful crowd control lies in the ability to judge when to let matters take their own course and when to get heavyhanded. (Something that is all too easily acquired in retrospect.) In this case, the arrival of the soldiers was doubly disastrous. While the presence of the soldiers acted as a magnet to the crowds it simultaneously discouraged the constables

– who felt that their authority was being undermined and usurped – from carrying out their policing duties.

The Chief Constable of St Nicholas Ward, Mr Neal, was one such person who had made himself scarce. On meeting the military in the High Street Mr Neal 'on a principle of self-preservation' turned on his heels and disappeared to the security of his own home[23].

The Riot Act was read, setting in motion a dreadful and inevitable sequence of events. In practice the Riot Act was not a particularly effective device for crowd control and was subject to all manner of vagaries. Basically, it warned that if after an hour any members of the crowd remained, they would be guilty of a capital offence. It also indemnified (at least in theory) the militia for any injury they caused by the violence they used. The implementation of the Riot Act also had other problems. In a large noisy gathering it was doubtful how many people could actually hear what was being read. Many innocent spectators did not understand that it referred to them as well as the obvious troublemakers. Additionally, in such a busy city thoroughfare it was just possible for people to pass by oblivious that they were challenging the law.

Although Mayor Henry Bengough was present, that night it was Alderman George Daubeny who was giving the orders. Time ticked by. St Nicholas's church clock struck eleven. Despite the lateness of the hour the crowd's size hardly diminished; a number of stones were thrown at the military and the magistrates. At 11.30 pm Alderman George Daubeny gave the order for the militia to fire above the heads of the crowd. It was a course of action that Mayor Bengough did not endorse. Muskets cracked, the people fled. 'Remember', said the Mayor, to no one in particular, 'they fired without my orders or consent'[24]. The crowd melted away to reveal a lone body lying on the ground, killed by a stray shot.

The Bristol Council House – situated on the corner of Corn Street and Broad Street – was a relatively small and unprepossessing building that was felt unworthy of such a great city. (City of Bristol Museum and Art Gallery)

Mayor Bengough's term of duty was due to come to an end the following day; his last full day in office must have been a time he would have liked to forget.

'LORD HAVE MERCY'

That evening, John Abbot, a builder's labourer, had gone to the *Ship Inn* in Redcliffe Street for a Saturday night drink. He also needed to obtain change – there was shortage of coins in circulation in the early 1790s – from the golden guinea that he and a fellow worker had jointly received for their wages. Abbot drank two pints of ale and then joined the crowd of spectators around the bridge. Just after 11.30 pm he was brought home, on the back of a man, wounded. He was in a state of delirium and was only able to cry repeatedly: 'Oh my God, I am death struck, Lord Jesus have mercy upon me.'

When his wife removed his breeches he began to bleed profusely. Medical aid was sought. After two doctors had refused to help, eventually Mr Salmon from Castle Green came to his aid. A ball had entered Abbot's left hip, penetrated his bowels and lodged in his spine. The doctor operated but was unable to remove the ball. John Abbot died shortly afterwards. He left a wife and two children[25].

'JUSTIFIABLE HOMICIDE'

The next day, the 29 September, was an important date in the Bristol calendar for it was then that the new civic year began. The change-over involved a procession to St Mark's Church (the Mayor's chapel) on College Green followed by the swearing-in of the new mayor and sheriffs in the Guildhall in Broad Street. The day started, however, at the Council House. The Council House, situated on the corner of Corn Street and Broad Street, was a relatively small and unprepossessing building. With its ornate Queen Anne features it looked like any other domestic house and was felt to be unworthy of the great Western Metropolis[26]. (It was rebuilt by the brilliant Robert Smirke, the architect of the British Museum, between 1824–7 and remains today substantially unaltered.) From the street visitors entered a large lobby. At the back of the lobby were the Mayor and Aldermen's rooms, whilst the council chambers were upstairs. The Mayor, along with several aldermen, was expected to be in attendance at the Council House between 12 noon and 3 pm everyday [27].

One of Mayor Bengough's last official duties was to pen a belated letter to the Secretary of State the Rt Hon. Henry Dundas requesting further help from the Military. Bengough, questioningly asked, in a roundabout manner 'whether a few troops of horse or Dragoons would not be the most efficacious?'[28].

Opinion in the Council House must have been divided regarding the effectiveness of the previous night's manoeuvres. On the one hand the deployment of the militia and their role in the dispersal of the crowd could be seen as a success. Of course, the death of a bystander was unfortunate, but the Riot Act had been read and the man had only himself to blame. On the other hand one could ask whether such force was really necessary? After all this was not a mob on the rampage and there was little evidence of more sinister undertones; the small number of active trouble-makers in the crowd appeared to be nothing more threatening than a bunch of high-spirited youngsters. Despite what was to be said later, it would take a very creative imagination to believe that the likes of Tom Paine and his fellow conspirators had been at work the previous night.

Whatever the view, one niggling question must have remained in many minds. The toll was not levied on those crossing by foot. Why, then, were the labouring poor protesting when they themselves didn't have to pay a penny of the toll?

As far as the majority of council members were concerned the disturbances 200 metres away down the hill on Bristol Bridge were merely an annoying distraction from the more serious matters of the day – the corporate ceremonies.

With the beginning of the new civic year it was an unusually busy Sunday in the Council House. And in the middle of all this pre-ceremony bustle two deputations, prompted by the previous night's events, arrived to speak to someone in authority. The first deputation, lead by John Chandler, a close relative (possibly brother-in-law) of John Abbott, arrived just before the Council went into recess. Chandler wished to enquire about the arrangements for the post-mortem on Abbot. The City Coroner, Joseph Safford, who was on hand for the civic ceremony explained that he did not intend to take the inquest that day, and indeed even when pressed, was reluctant to specify when he would carry it out. Dissatisfied with this vagueness, Chandler, next questioned Alderman Ames who was passing through the lobby at the time. Ames said that they would have to wait until the Chief Magistrate arrived. Not to be put off, Chandler sought out Mayor Bengough. Without hesitation the Mayor summoned Safford and ordered him to undertake the inquest as soon as possible. Bengough also asserted – and this surprised even Safford – that the verdict would be:

'Justifiable homicide, for the Riot Act had been read.' He also added hastily: 'Though I did not read it myself – Mr Daubeny did.'

Safford was startled at this flagrant challenge to his professional impartiality and queried this assertion. The Mayor, however, assured Safford that a number of officers could swear to it. The town clerk, Mr George Merrick, was called to give witness to this fact[29].

(Later on, however, the jury at the coroner's enquiry were not so easily influenced. The coroner did his best to keep proceedings short[30] but the jury would have none of it. Having sat for seven hours they plainly rejected the Mayor's wishes and much to Safford's chagrin returned the damning verdict of 'Wilful murder against a person or personsunknown.'[31])

A second deputation, representing a group of concerned residents who lived in close vicinity to the Bridge, arrived at 10.30 am. By this time the Common Council was in recess, and as Mayor Bengough only had an hour and a half in office to serve, there seemed little point in calling him out of the proceedings. Although they went away empty-handed they were assured by an official that these troubled times were high on the council's agenda[32].

Despite the growing anxiety over law and order, the morning's civic ceremonies went ahead undisturbed and with full pomp and splendour James Morgan, a druggist from Corn Street, was sworn into office as Bristol's new mayor and chief magistrate.

'NO TOLL! NO TOLL! NO TOLL!'

The real test of the Bridge Commissioner's resolve came at midday when men were posted on the bridge in readiness to collect the toll. On hand to see that the toll was collected and that all was in order was George Daubeny. At noon, immediately, the toll was enforced a group of men who had been idling by the bridge moved into action. Within seconds there was a small crowd jostling toll collectors and toll-payers alike. Tempers quickly rose; the magistrates were goaded by the crowd; toll-payers were bewildered; horses were frightened. The parish constables, this time there were several in attendance, appeared powerless – and reluctant – to do anything. For those who wished to cross the bridge it was difficult to know what to do. Was the toll legally enforceable? Should they pay? Or should they give over to the intimidation of the mob? A coachman who drove his horses over the bridge from the Redcliffe side was besieged by the crowd. While the constables moved forward to collect the toll the demonstrators urged him to drive straight on. Deciding to retreat rather than become embroiled in the debate the coachman started to back-up his horses. At this point Alderman George Daubeny's composure cracked: in an undignified and provocative manner he reached up and grabbed the horse's reins. The driver, alarmed at this attack by an unknown assailant, lashed out with his whip. In retaliation Daubeny grabbed the man and pulled him to the ground[33]. Daubeny's behaviour was doing his credibility as a peacemaker – and that of the Corporation – no good at all. At a time like this a calming influence was needed – something that was not being supplied by Daubeny. The presence of the militia, who were summoned after several ineffectual readings of the Riot Act, did impose some sort of short-term equilibrium upon the crowd. Against a chant of 'No toll! No toll! No toll!' the toll-collectors were able to get on with their business. Indeed, the atmosphere was relaxed enough for Lord Bateman, the Colonel in Chief of the Hereford Militia to mingle with the crowd and listen to the views of a number of gentlemen spectators regarding the toll's unpopularity and its supposed illegality[34]. Yet, to many, the very presence of the militia was a puzzle. What exactly was their role in all this? Were they expected to merely stand and watch? Following the debacle of the previous evening the feeling was that however many times the Riot Act was read the militia were unlikely to be ordered to use force. Others suggested that their muskets were merely charged with blanks. Such talk was to prove fatally misleading. As dusk fell, the magistrates, the constables and the militia marched off and allowed free passage of the bridge. For the Corporation it had been a difficult and trying day; far worse was yet to come, however.

Notes

1. Rosser, p.6. cf. E. John *'Saturday Night's Alright for Fighting."*
2. Hall, I.V., The Daubenys, Bristol and Gloucestershire Archaeological Society 1965, p.114-5.
3. Latimer, p.446.
4. Petition posted March 12 1781 to House of Commons against the return of George Daubeny. B.R.L., B.8774.
5. Hall I.V., *The Daubenys,* Bristol and Gloucestershire Archaeological Society 1965, p.113-40.
6. He was called this in the anonymous pamphlet *'A Chapter out of the book of Morgan'* (undated, probably Autumn 1793), B.R.L. B 25372, p.2.
7. Matthews, p.90.
8. Thompson E.P., *Making of the English Working Class* (1979), p.85.
9. Jones, P.D., *The Bristol Bridge Riot and Its Antecedents: Eighteenth Century Perception of the Crowd,* Journal of British Studies, XlX, 2, 1980, pp.74-82.
10. Colley, L., *Britons – Forging the Nation 1707-1837* (London, 1994) p.35.
11. Bristol Record Society Publication Vol. XL, *Bristol Gaol Fiats 1741-1799,* (1989) ed. George Lamoine p.113.
12. Rude, G., *The Crowd in History 1730-1848* (London 1985) p.34.
13. Latimer, p.373.
14. Latimer, p.447.
15. Evans, J., *A Chronological Outline of the History of Bristol,* (1824), p.272.
16. Rude,G., *The Crowd in History 1730-1848* (London 1985) p.40.
17. Latimer p.378.
18. Committee, pp.26-9.
19. Gilmour, I., *Riot, Risings and Revolution* (London 1992) p.294.
20. Latimer J., p.322.
21. B.R.O Town Clerk's Box for 1793.
22. Rose p.7-8. Rosser p.7.

23. Committee p.44.
24. Committee, p.16.
25. Committee, pp 9-13.
26. For an illustration of the Old Council House see Ison W., *The Georgian Buildings of Bristol* (1952) p.91.
27. Matthews, p.81.
28. *Town Clerk's Letter Book,* 29 September 1793 p.43. B. R. O. 05158.
29. Committee, pp.16-18.
30. Committee, p.37.
31. Committee, p.18.
32. Committee, pp.23-4.
33. Rose, p.9.
34. Rose, p.9.

FIVE

Bloody Monday

The working day was in full swing, when at 9.00 am, a chain was pulled across the Bristol Bridge roadway in lieu of gates. All carts, carriages, pack horses and other modes of transport wishing to cross the River Avon were forced to an immediate standstill. With an estimated 60 people a minute crossing the bridge at peak times the traffic in the surrounding streets quickly backed-up and became congested[1]. Within minutes movement in the centre of Bristol had come to a complete halt.

What happened next was all very predictable; Mr Symons yet again summoned help. First of all from the civil power – the magistrates, the parish constables and their assistants – and then the militia. George Daubeny, one of two magistrates on the scene, appeared to be at his wit's end. He was in a more subdued mood than on the previous day and even attempted to give the crowd a short sermon based on an Aesop fable. He drew a parallel between himself and the bugle boy who could not be held responsible for the charge of the cavalry. The moral of this ambiguous story seemed to have more to do with Daubeny absolving himself of liability for public injury, than clearing the on-lookers. Daubeny was having trouble sorting out his own interests from his civic responsibilities. Needless to say his oratory had absolutely no effect on the crowd. In the space of half an hour, between 10.30 am and 11.00 am, the Riot Act was read three times[2]. The crowd was warned that 'those that will not be advised must take the consequences, and that if they receive any injury it must be upon their own heads.' But then, when the militia arrived nothing happened; no action was taken. The magistrates were sending out the wrong messages. The longer the militia stood passively around the more ambiguous their role became. Dangerous rumours continued to circulate that the militia were not allowed to fire[3]. In the eyes of the crowd the militia had become as impotent as toy soldiers.

George Daubeny's mood began to change; his moment of calm had passed and he now seemed to be in a higher state of frenzy than on the previous day – if that were possible. He was an easy target for the taunts of the crowd, returning abuse with abuse. At one stage he dragged – by all accounts – an innocent man out of the crowd and had him pulled by his feet all the way up the hill to Newgate Gaol.

The other magistrate on duty was none other than John Noble, the former mayor who had made such a show of himself at the Old Bailey. John Noble's manner was equally belligerent. His aggressive stance was typified by a recent handbill issued under his name, whereby he baited the Bridge Commissioner's critics with accusations of cowardliness and opportunism.

If anyone wishes to have a general account stated, or each year particularised; I request you to make your desire known, not by anonymous unmanly letters, but by such a public manly request, properly signed, as will shew your fellow citizens, and the world at large, that you only want to be justified as to the management of the Tax, not desirous of supporting disorder, tumult and riot[4].

Such a combative reply hardly encouraged rational debate and must only have served to heighten tension. And despite all previous requests, the Bridge Commissioners were still reluctant to itemise their accounts.

John Noble's own public behaviour was equally inflammatory – at times he seemed almost to be sparing for a fight. In a scene which would have been farcical had it not been so tragic Noble accosted some men who were carrying an empty coffin over the bridge towards Redcliffe. As the coffin bearers halted briefly on the bridge for a rest Noble stormed over to them shouting that they stopped at their own peril. A nearby soldier asked who the coffin was for.

'For the man murdered on Saturday night,' replied Chandler, one of the coffin bearers.

At this Noble flew into a rage.

'So that's what you think, is it?', Noble bellowed.

Chandler affirmed that it was.

'Then Sir, I am determined to mark you,' threatened Noble. 'I know you very well indeed.'

And, at this, he stormed off[5].

Many were still not convinced that the toll was legally enforceable and were reluctant to pay. The Corporation was sending out no clear message and it was impossible to know who was representing whom. Was George Daubeny acting in his capacity as a magistrate? Or as a Bridge Trustee? Likewise John Noble. At one stage George Daubeny was even seen to be actively collecting tolls; this was not the impartial behaviour expected – well, hoped for – of a magistrate.

As dusk approached the toll booths were closed down for the night and the fifty soldiers were ordered to march back to their quarters[6]. Sensing a small victory, the trouble makers increased their harassment of the soldiers as they marched through the crowd on their way to the Council House. The commanding officer was involved in a scuffle and hit on the back of the head as he tried to arrest one of his assailants.

The situation now took an unexpected turn for the worse and

despite the soldiers' departure a more sinister momentum started to take a grip. The size of the crowd began to grow to alarming proportions. Although the spectators had been substantial on previous days the crowd on this Monday evening was enormous. The roads were jammed with a sea of onlookers; young and old, men and women filled the streets. It seemed as if all Bristol had turned out to see what was going on. In an age when the biggest crowd-puller was an execution, the unfolding of events on the bridge were, without doubt, riveting entertainment. And although the vast majority of people knew it was unwise to be there – handbills warning that the Riot Act had been read had been hastily produced on the Bristol Mercury press and distributed – they were nevertheless drawn to the spectacle like moths to a lamp. As Monday's work finished – even though it was a dark and cloudy night – spectators assembled at all the best viewing points. To the north of the bridge on a triangle of land in front of St. Nicholas' church; along Welsh Back and Bridge Street – all these places offered good vantage points. To the south of the river the view was more restricted. Even so, people gathered along Bath Street and hung out of every well-appointed window. Some even climbed onto roofs. The stage was set and the audience was ready for some first class entertainment.

As soon as the soldiers departed a number of young men ran to Welsh Back to collect faggots. The brand new tollgates, barely hours old, were yet again the centre of an inferno[7]. Then as the fire burnt out the toll house door was knocked down and chairs, tables, an old sentry box, besoms, even the constable's brass headed staves were heaped, in high-spirited fun, onto the fire[8]. With the crowd singing 'God Save the King' the mood in the vicinity of the bridge was that of carnival and celebration.

Meanwhile, up at the Council House, one can guess these events were being interpreted from a very different perspective. A mob like this could only mean trouble: *agent provocateurs* were stirring the people up; Bristol's own *sans culottes* were being mobilised; there was also talk of the rabble enlisting help from the colliers and freeing the French prisoners from the Stapleton Gaol. Riot, even revolution, was in the air[9].

Two peace officers were sent to observe the mood of the masses. Then, for reasons that have never satisfactorily been explained – perhaps they were testing the mood – a small squad of eight soldiers, headed by Captain Maxwell, was dispatched to the bridge. With a cry of 'The soldiers!' the score (Rosser says 100) of young men stoking the fire disappeared into the safety of the crowd. It quickly became apparent, however, that as the militia were unaccompanied by any magistrates, they were powerless to act. The troublemakers became more adventurous. While the unfortunate soldiers remained on the bridge they were an easy and defenceless target for anyone inclined to hurl a missile at them. Oyster shells from the fish stalls on Welsh Back, stones, brickbats and clods of mud rained down on them. Captain Maxwell was hit on the head and his hat was knocked off. After a just a few minutes of this humiliation the soldiers beat a hasty retreat[10].

At 8.15 pm, a second larger detachment of soldiers, this time headed by the Mayor, five Aldermen and some peace officers left the Council House[11]. Accompanied by fife and drum the soldiers marched along the High Street passing first of all on the left the rambling half-timbered Dutch House and then on the right the elegant palladian entrance to the market. In just two minutes they arrived at the Bridge. James Morgan, now only into the second day of his new position, appeared to be keeping a low profile and leaving the orders to the old hands – though whether this inaction was by choice it was difficult to tell. Children in the crowd were hoisted onto shoulders to get a better view. By the expression on the soldier's faces it looked like they meant business. They had suffered many hours of abuse silently. Now, with bayonets fixed and their muskets loaded the soldiers were ready for action. The crowd's mood of exhilaration changed to apprehension. Some members of the crowd were still enjoying the aggravation – as the soldiers stopped halfway across the bridge they were met by a hail of missiles. Crouching on one knee, the soldiers assumed the firing position. The beat of the drum changed to an ominous roll. The enormous concourse of people became hushed with expectation; the noise of the shouting crowd subsided to a murmur, and then became silent.

The precise details of what happened next, and who gave the command to fire is unclear; after the event no one was publicly willing to admit responsibility. Even to those standing nearby the order to fire was barely audible above the sound of the drums. With no further warning the soldiers fired southwards straight along St Thomas Street. They were doing the unthinkable. No Riot Act had been read since the morning, no other methods of crowd control had been tried. Admittedly, although there were numerous books on drill and the theory of war, not a word had, at that time, been written about crowd control and riots[12]. But even so the next logical step should have been a bayonet charge. A volley into the crowd, and a crowd such as this, was a last resort.

Although the overall size of the crowd was large, amounting to several thousands, the number of active participants was small, perhaps no more than fifty in all at any one time. The role of the vast majority of the crowd was passive – it was only a few troublemakers, all young and male that went on the rampage. And yet, despite the current lack of work, despite the widespread vogue for 'liberty', despite what the Corporation would imply later, these were not revolutionaries on the rampage. In comparison with some of the mob events that had recently occurred in France, the behaviour of the Bristol Bridge crowd looked muted. There were no obvious ringleaders and damage to property was strictly confined to possessions of the Bridge Trustees. At no time did the energy of the crowd redirect itself to other targets. In short, the mob was neither inspired by Paine's simple rhetoric, nor was it acting out Burke's nightmarish predictions.

Muskets cracked, shots sliced through the air. People tried to take cover; they desperately sought shelter in doorways or behind projecting window-bays – anywhere that offered some protection. But the crowded streets made this difficult, several fell over and were trampled upon.

Gunsmoke and the sweet scorched smell of gunpowder hung in the night air over the bridge.

Despite their volleys southwards, the soldiers continued to be attacked from the north in the direction of the High Street[13]. Perhaps their assailants still believed that blanks were being fired. The back rank of soldiers was ordered to about turn and fire directly into the crowd. In almost every direction people were shot by the musketry. Shots travelled as far as the High Street junction with Wine Street (afterwards the owner of the shop with a curved frontage tucked into the south west corner of Christchurch – it is still there today – displayed a neat shot hole in one of his window panes). One soldier reloaded his musket and cold-bloodedly took a second shot at a man who had already fallen. On the south side of the bridge the soldiers broke rank. In Redcliffe Street a soldier, sword in hand, entered a house in hot pursuit of rioters. Outside other soldiers drew up in a half moon shape in front of the building. They only refrained from shooting into the house after desperate pleading from the owner.

Shortly after the firing the military left the bridge. The night was remarkably dark. In all, over 100 rounds had been fired. At 11 pm a heavy shower of rain washed away every trace of blood.

...

With the street lamps broken it was an impenetrably dark night. On his way home, Matthew Bennet tripped over a large object on the ground. It was the body of a young man, flat on his back, cold and quite dead. To his utter disbelief Bennet realised that he was staring at a corpse – the corpse of his own son, James.

This long horrible moment was broken by Joseph Horler, the Mayor's secretary, striding up to the bereaved father. Horler, who appeared to be in an exceptionally agitated mood, demanded:

'Who is this fellow?'

Bennet was so distraught that he could hardly speak.

'It is my son,' he cried.

'Damn ye,' said Horler. 'Take him away directly, or I assure you that worse will ensue'[14].

A LIST of PERSONS *Killed* and *Wounded*

(At the late RIOTS in BRISTOL refpecting the *Bridge Tolls*,)

On the memorable Evening of the *30th* of September, *1793*,

In Confequence of the FIRE from the MILITARY;

With the VERDICTS returned by the Coroners' Inquefts;

AND

Their AGES, Defcription of their WOUNDS, &c.

A LIST OF THE KILLED.

JOHN ABBOTT, aged 55, Tiler and Plaifterer.—Verdict, Wilful Murder by Perfon or Perfons unknown.

William Aldridge.—Verdict, Wilful Murder by Perfon or Perfons unknown.

James Howell, Parifh of St. James, aged 28, Mafon.—Verdict, Wilful Murder by Perfon or Perfons unknown.

William Powell, of Caftle Precincts, Baker.—Verdict, Wilful Murder by Perfon or Perfons unknown. [The firft Verdict returned by the Jury fworn to inquire the Caufe of this Gentleman's Death, was "Wilful Murder by the Perfon who ordered the Military to fire," which Verdict the Coroner refufed to receive; and the Jurors were, after fome time, induced to return a fecond Verdict, as above.]

Thomas Morgan.—Verdict, Wilful Murder by Perfon or Perfons unknown.

Humphrey Lewis, of Caftle-Carey.—Verdict, Wilful Murder by Perfon or Perfons unknown.

John Jones, Accomptant.—Verdict, Wilful Murder by Perfon or Perfons unknown.

Anthony Gill, Shoemaker, Parifh of St. James, aged 34.—Verdict, Wilful Murder by Perfon or Perfons unknown.

James Bennet, aged 22, Parifh of St. Mary Redcliff.—Verdict, Accidental Death.

Isaac Davis, aged 18, Parifh of St. Thomas.—Verdict, Wilful Murder by Perfon or Perfons unknown.

Elizabeth Kegan, aged 55, Parifh of St. Stephen.—Verdict, Wilful Murder by Perfon or Perfons unknown.

A LIST OF THE WOUNDED.

OF REDCLIFF PARISH.

Harriet Davis, aged 13, gun-fhot wound in the Thigh.
Sarah Silcox, aged 55, wound in the Thigh.
Eliz. Hithens, aged 16, wound in the Foot.
Dan. Bishop, aged 20, wound in the Arm.
Jane Thomas, aged 18, wound in the Foot.
Stephen Cox, aged 19, wound in the Thigh.

OF TEMPLE PARISH.

Joseph White, aged 44, gun-fhot wound in the Side.
Henry Knotley, aged 24, wound in the Leg and Arm.
Thomas Knotley, aged 22, wound in the Thighs.
Caleb Love, aged 51, amputated Arm.
Richard Ponsford, aged 32, wound in the Thigh.
Thomas Stephens, aged 18, wound in the Thigh.
Thomas Smith, aged 23, wound in the Leg.
Michael Nelson, aged 22, wound in the Head.
John Alexander, aged 42, wound through the Leg.
William Davis, aged 22, wound in the Ancle.
Robert Hughes, aged 18, wound in the Shoulder.

OF ST. THOMAS PARISH.

William Thomson, aged 29, gun-fhot wound in the Arm.
Richard Cole, aged 17, wound in the Thigh.
Mary Knight, aged 46, wound in the Foot.

OF THE PARISH OF ST. PHILIP AND JACOB.

Esther Nash, aged 19, gun-fhot wound in the Leg.
John Hookins, aged 19, wound in the Thigh.
James Jarrett, aged 22, wound in the Shoulder.
Benjamin Parish, aged 45, wound in the Hand.
Samuel Hopkins, aged 23, wound in the Face.

OF THE PARISH OF ST. JAMES.

Thomas Powell, aged 18, gun-fhot wound in the Head.
William Anstice, aged 21, wound in the Hand.
Thomas Hedgland, aged 34, wound in the Hand.
Malachi Norris, aged 43, contufed Eye.
Thomas Rossiter, aged 45, grazed Forehead.

OF THE PARISH OF ST. STEPHEN.

—— *Davis*, aged 50, gun-fhot wound in the Knee.
Thomas Coles, aged 38, wound in the Leg.

OF THE PARISH OF ST. NICHOLAS.

William Puddicomb, aged 32, gun-fhot wounds in the Wrift and Hip.
Margaret Morgan, aged 49, wound in the Heel.
William Burleigh, aged 14, wound in the Foot.
William Wrestill, aged 28, Parifh of St. *Maryport*, gun-fhot wound in the Legs.
William Horwood, aged 20, Parifh of St. *George*, gun-fhot wounds in the Groin and Hand.
Charles Coole, aged 25, Parifh of *Bitton*, gun-fhot wound in the Abdomen.
William Graves, aged 20, Parifh of St. *Paul*, gun-fhot wound in the Wrift.
John Lloyd, aged 17, gun-fhot wound in the Face.
Daniel Pierce, aged about 15, gun-fhot wounds in the Foot and Heel.
Thomas Baynham, aged about 26, fabre wound in the Hand.
Thomas Foxall, aged about 17, *Bridgnorth*, bayonet wound in the Hand.
Thomas Parke, aged about 27, gun-fhot wound through the Shoulder.
William Alwick, aged about 27, gun-fhot wound through the Thigh.
Henry Edminston, aged about 35, gun-fhot wound through the Arm.
James Edwards, aged about 32, gun-fhot wound in the Leg.
Robert Hewett, aged about 40, gun-fhot wound in the Face.
Thomas Rogers, aged about 42, gun-fhot wound in the Loin.
James Harris, aged about 23, gun-fhot wound in the Knee.
John Kingdom, aged about 22, Parifh of *Bedminster*, gun-fhot wounds in the Hand and Thigh.
—— *Jenkins*, aged about 29, Parifh of St. *Peter*, gun-fhot wound in the Shoulder.

N. B. Several of the Wounded have fince Died.

[Price TWO-PENCE.]

A List of Persons Killed and Wounded. It had been a busy night at the Bristol Infirmary on 30 September 1793 as the injured were brought for treatment by cart, wheelbarrow or whatever was at hand. Bristol Infirmary records show that three of those listed as injured died later. Five weeks after the massacre the total number of fatal casualties had risen to 14. (Bristol Reference Library)

Notes

1. This estimate was made by John Rose – even if the figure was not scientifically calculated it does nevertheless give a feel for the sheer volume of traffic that crossed the bridge on a daily basis. Rose, p.11.
2. Rosser, p.8.
3. Rosser, p.11.
4. Handbill, signed by John Noble and dated September 30 1793, Mardon Collection BRL B.11539.
5. Committee, p.19.
6. Rosser gives the time as 7.00 pm. Rosser, p.8.
7. Rosser, p.8.
8. Rosser, p.9.
9. Mr Seyer's Manuscripts, p.43.
10. Rosser, p.11.
11. Rosser, p.11.
12. Gilmour, I., *Riots, Risings and Revolution* (London 1992) p.144.
13. Rosser, p.11.
14. Committee, p.25-6.

SIX

'Murder by person, or persons unknown'

The next morning as the bodies of the dead were laid out and the number of wounded counted, the true scale of the massacre became apparent. Eleven were registered as dead, and approximately forty-five injured[1]. Twenty-eight wounded were received at the Infirmary, several of whom had to undergo amputations[2]. As the city coroners, Joseph Safford Jnr and Thomas Parker, undertook their rounds (under these circumstances they had no opportunity to procrastinate) it became increasingly obvious that, with one exception, those gunned down were not hooligans but well respected, hard-working members of the community.

During the euphoria of the previous night the 'mob' had taken on an almost abstract form – now in the cold light of day, when senses had been regained, it was all too obvious that the crowd was made up of individuals, real people of flesh and blood. Included in the list of the dead were a number of tradesmen, one woman, Elizabeth Keegan from St Stephen's Parish and a traveller from Castle Cary[3]. During their brief inquests, held in a number of taverns and inns in the central parishes, witnesses repeatedly gave testament as to the respectability of the deceased: that the victims were returning home; that they had only joined the crowd to see what was going on; that they were *not* rioters.The coroners returned a verdict on one person of 'accidental death'; of the remaining ten the verdict was a damning 'murder by person or persons unknown'. Even more damning, had

COUNCIL-HOUSE,

BRISTOL, 3d *October*, 1793.

THE MAGISTRATES of the City do hereby call upon *all Fathers of Families*, to inſtruct their *Children* not to be loitering about the Streets and joining with idle Perſons;---upon *all Maſters* to command their *Servants*;---upon *all Tradeſmen and Manufacturers* to exhort their *Labourers* to paſs quietly and peaceably along the Streets of this City, and not to join with the Riotous and Diſorderly in abuſing, throwing Dirt, or otherwiſe inſulting any of the Military, *who have only done their Duty*. The MAGISTRATES having given the ſtricteſt Order to all their Peace-Officers, and do hereby call upon all *good Citizens* to aſſiſt in apprehending ſuch Diſturbers of the public Peace, who will be dealt by with the utmoſt Severity of the Law.

WORRALL, *Town-Clerk.*

This handbill issued by the Council House called for restraint and a return to law and order. Although the Council promised that the 'disturbers of the public peace' would be dealt with severely, in the end only one person was brought before the magistrates – for shouting abuse at Lord Bateman in Park Street. (Bristol Reference Library) the coroners allowed it, would have been the verdict of the jury who investigated the body of Mr Powell.

Their first verdict 'wilful murder by the person or persons who ordered the militia to fire' clearly censured the magistrates and must surely have been a matter of deep concern for the, as yet, un-named culprit[4]. For the Mayor and the magistrates the question was what to do next. Right across the spectrum of political belief there was a creeping sense of outrage among the citizens of Bristol. Even the Corporation's most ardent supporters had to admit that something had gone very seriously wrong. The death of eleven people and the injury of countless others was an unacceptable price to pay for the enforcement of law and order. Moreover, as reports appeared in newspapers across the land, what had started as a local disturbance was now turning into a national scandal. Was there to be no end to it?

In an attempt to put the record straight the Corporation hastily issued a short broadsheet summarising their perspective of the previous night's events. Signed by Sam Worral, the Town Clerk, on behalf of the Mayor and Aldermen, the handbill briefly outlined events and pointed out that the common people should have no cause to complain about the toll 'as they pay it not, but only the substantial citizens, householders, manufacturers, and merchants and gentry who travel over the Bridge.' Even so the Corporation did have the good grace to concede that:

The consequence (much to be lamented as it undoubtedly is) has been that several persons have been killed and wounded, some of whom it is very probable, may have been innocent without any evil intention themselves...

In conclusion, however, Worral added that such innocents were:

indiscrete and blameable in adding to the multitude by their individual presence, after being forewarned by printed handbills, distributed about the town by the discretion of the magistrates, which handbills informed the citizens that the Riot Act had been read and that the military would be desired to fire if the riotous did not disperse.

And that, as far as the Corporation was concerned, was the end of the matter.

'OH, WHAT MISERY IN BAD HANDS'

It was now the turn of the people to ask what was going on. A sense of indignation and injustice raged across the city. How could members of the Corporation, the so-called representatives of the people, order the militia to gun down their own kin-folk? Who was in charge? Who should shoulder the blame? This sense of fear, bewilderment and misapprehension is exemplified by an extraordinary and emotive letter sent anonymously to William Pitt, the Prime Minister, on 3 October 1793.

My Dear Sir,

Help us to have justice. Our streets are filled with the murdered bodies of the inhabitants. The most wanton cruelty have been exercised by Lord Batman's soldiers...we should have no disturbance was it not for the Corporation. Help us, help us kind Gracious Sir, We shall all be murdered...For Gods sake send us some help or some person that is human. George Daubeny has brought this misery on a people peaceably inclined and firmly attached to his majesty and the present constitution by a show of justice...I have wrote to the King and long may he live...Do pray send some person. They are now at the Guildhall going to fire again. We shall be murdered. Indeed Sir, we shall. They have so enraged the people...O what misery in bad hands. God bless you and all the faithful servants of the King. God be merciful to his poor wretched creatures'[5].

Although the handwriting of this poignant letter is in places indecipherable, this train of free-flowing thought describes a world turned upside-down. The writer saw a power-mad Daubeny and Corporation going to absolute extremes to cow the people into submission. There was no mention of radicals or revolutionaries attempting to overturn the establishment. Far from it, it was the King's loyal subjects that were being slain on their own streets.

The Hereford militia meanwhile had been confined to quarters for their own safety at the Guildhall. During the evening a crowd assembled on the bridge and then made its way up the hill to Broad Street. First the windows of the Guildhall and then those of the Council House were shattered by an enraged populace looking for some small measure of revenge. With no other targets to attack the people then dispersed[6]. A handbill was issued from the Council House calling upon:

Fathers of families, to instruct their Children not to be loitering about the streets and joining with idle persons; upon all masters to command their servants; upon all tradesmen and manufacturers to exhort their labourers to pass quietly along the streets of the city, and not to join the riotous and disorderly in abusing, throwing dirt or other wise insulting the military, who have only done their duty[7].

Members of the Corporation had manoeuvred themselves into an impossible situation. They could not back down, they had to stick to their guns. In order to muster further support, James Morgan and Alderman Sir John Durbin sent a note to the Chief Constable of each ward requesting them to immediately summon the principal inhabitants of their parish in order to consider any further measures that could be taken to support the policing of the city[8]. In the afternoon Morgan also wrote to the Duke of Beaufort requesting that he send reinforcements *immediately.* With unintentional irony, Morgan predicted that violence from the crowd was imminent. He wrote that the previous night's show of force had 'not produced the desired effect, for great numbers of riotous persons are at this moment again collecting and threatening to commit still greater outrages'. Morgan finished his letter by ominously recommending 'that the troops be provided with ammunition on entering Bristol'[9].

Reinforcements in the shape of the Monmouthshire Militia and the First regiment of Dragoon guards arrived in Bristol on Wednesday 2 October[10]. During the evening the Dragoons paraded the streets with their swords drawn. They had no cause, however, to use their muskets. The immediate anger of the crowd had burnt itself out. 'Everything is quiet now,' wrote John Rose, 'tho' the public mind is deeply affected'[11].

Yet the ordeal was not over for several of the more unfortunate casualties. It had been a busy night at the Bristol Infirmary on 30 September as the injured were brought for treatment by cart, wheelbarrow or whatever was on hand. While many were discharged over the next few days, several were not so fortunate. As the weeks went by the number of dead slowly grew.

Bristol was indeed lucky to have its Infirmary. It had recently been rebuilt and was able to provide beds for 150 in-patients. It also had a particularly enlightened management who proclaimed 'that all persons, without regard to country, colour or dialect, who are accidentally injured, are on application immediately admitted, without any recommendation whatsoever'. Of course, treatment of the ill was rudimentary and not always for the best. For some inexplicable reason the walls of the Infirmary were all coated with black plaster which gave it an 'extremely lugubrious appearance'[12].

Examination of Bristol Infirmary's records show that three of those listed by John Rose as being injured died later[13]. William Puddicombe succumbed to his gunshot wounds in the head and hip on 26 October; Joseph White, who had received a gun-shot wound to his side, died two days later, while Thomas Coles who had been shot in the arm died on 2 November. So, five weeks after the massacre, the total number of fatal casualties had risen to 14.

'PUBLIC TRANQUILLITY' IS RESTORED.

The official reaction to the disturbances on the bridge is remarkable in that there was no official reaction. Beyond, as we have seen, the issue of the short statement pointing out that the burden of the toll did not fall on the common people[14] and the warning to keep off the streets[15] there was a determined effort to play down the reason for the troubles. The Corporation refused to hold an enquiry into the events, their justification for this being that a formal investigation would offer further opportunity for the 'revolutionaries' to stir-up trouble. In wartime such 'concessions' to the people could not be allowed.

Additionally, despite the lack of any hard evidence, there was talk of a wider-reaching republican plot to undermine those in command. This was a particularly devious tack to follow; it not only played on the fears of the citizens but it was also extremely difficult to disprove. Indeed, as was to happen, an accusing finger could be pointed at anyone who was thought to be challenging the authorities. Thus in a letter to the Henry Dundas, the Home Secretary, dated 7 October, the Mayor wrote that the instigators of the disturbances 'had other objectives besides putting a stop to the collection of the Bridge Toll'[16]. Morgan added that 'the Magistrates are now using their best endeavours to discover and bring to justice the instigators of these disturbances...'[17]

Members of the Corporation were walking a difficult line. Publically, they had to be seen to be doing their utmost to track down the troublemakers; privately, the last thing they wanted was a series of trials where their actions would come under the scrutiny. If the coroner's inquests were anything to go by the wisdom of the course of action taken by the Corporation would be open to question. Other irregularities were also likely to be exposed. For example, on whose authority had the troops been called out on the night of the 28 September? Why had Henry Bengough written retrospectively to the Home Secretary requesting permission to bring in the militia? Both Mayors Bengough and Morgan, along with any other magistrates deemed responsible, could, if they were not very careful indeed, be facing prosecution for murder. Thus, despite the issue and display of numerous public notices offering rewards for information leading to conviction, only one man was brought before the justices at the December Quarter Sessions, and that was merely for shouting abuse at Lord Bateman and his soldiers as they marched up Park Street.

Even the *Minute Book of the Proceedings of the Common Council* is suspiciously lacking in any direct reference to the troubles. Whilst

Bristol was on the verge of burning it appears that the city councillors were calmly discussing the price of turbot[18].

Even so, how do we explain the incendary behaviour of the young? Despite the general assertion that at the end of the eighteenth century riots were the most common form of popular politics[19], in this case analysis indicates that the word 'disturbance' would be a more appropriate description of events. Admittedly, prices were rising, as was unemployment – yet these issues were never aired as grievances. Certainly this was no overt class unrest and despite the innuendo of the Corporation there were no real indications of any revolutionary or radical agitation.

Perhaps the behaviour of the troublemaking element of the crowd can be put down to youthful exuberance inflamed by drink and an audience that appeared to support their anti-establishment behaviour. Is this disrespect of authority the key? The historian, Mark Harrison, has suggested that the protests against the toll were in fact a tangible way of the people expressing their overall disapproval of the Corporation[20]. As Harrison points out, many sections of the crowd were actively encouraging the troublemakers. In short the toll was a side issue – it was merely acting as a catalyst for the expression of a deep-seated resentment of the Corporation.

In the end the dispute over the toll was settled with remarkable and unexpected speed. The troubles did at least galvanise one group of people into action. A consortium of prominent businessmen including John Bally, William Elton, John Thomas and Matthew Wright[21] (none of whom were Common Council members) made an offer to the Bridge Commissioners of £1,920 to cover any debts that were owing. The group made it known that they would accept contributions from the public to help them with their payment (they also optimistically stated that if that if they received any more than the required amount it would be donated to the Infirmary)[22]. The rationale for this charitable intervention is unrecorded, yet without diminishing noble motives of goodwill, common sense and a feeling that enough was enough, it should be pointed out that for several days Bristol's traffic, and consequently Bristol's trade had been at a standstill. From a straightforward economic point of view, especially during such hard times, this disruption could not be allowed to continue.

James Morgan, George Daubeny, and John Noble could hardly disguise their contempt at this perceived acquiescence to the rule of the mob. The magistrates unanimously issued a warning that 'it was not a wise or salutory measure'. They also cautioned that 'after the outrages that have been committed, (it) may be considered a concession on the part of the Police of the city, which may be attended with serious consequences in the future'[23].

The outcome of the emergency ward meetings was not entirely encouraging for the Corporation. While all the parishes expressed bland platitudes of support and offered whatever help they could to restore order, some were outrightly critical of the Corporation. The people of St Mary's censured the Bridge Commissioners for 'letting the tolls for a whole year when it does not appear that more than three months income was necessary to compleat the purposes of the act'; the people of St Nicholas criticised the use of the military; three parishes even voiced their support for the consortium who had paid-off the debt. Paraphrasing the words of the Corporation, the representatives of Temple Ward went so far as to write that their actions were 'neither unwise, nor improper – indeed they were absolutely necessary'. For members of the Corporation these replies were disturbing news and a further indication of how public opinion – indeed the opinion of the 'principal citizens' – was against them[24].

While the settlement of accounts may have signalled the end of the Bristol Bridge Toll, the accusations of murder and maladministration – and a local population hungry for revenge – still remained.

Notes

1. *A List of persons Killed and Wounded (At the late Riots in Bristol respecting the Bridge Tolls)* B.R.L. A slightly different list is also appended to Rose's Impartial History.
2. Bonner & Middleton's *Bristol Journal*, 5 October 1793.
3. Rose, pp.15-6.
4. Rose, p.15.
5. Public Record Office H.042/26. The spelling and punctuation are mine. I am indebted to Mark Harrison in *'Raise and Dare Resentment': the Bristol Bridge Riot of 1793.* Historical Journal 26, 3 (1983), p.583 for indicating this source.
6. Rosser, p.15.
7. *Handbill from the Council House*, dated 3rd October 1793, signed by Worral. B.R.L. B.13074.
8. B.R.O. *Town Clerk's Box* 1793.
9. Bristol Record Office, *Town Clerk's Letter Book* (05158) p.44.
10. Rosser p.15.
11. Rose p.14.
12. Latimer p.480.
13. B.R.O FCH/BRI/3(h)11
14. *Narrative of facts of the proceedings of yesterday in the city of Bristol* (BCRL B.13074)
15. Worral, *Council House, Bristol* 3rd October 1793 BCRL B.13074
16. Bristol Record Office, *Town Clerk's Letter Book* (05158) October 7 1793
17. Bristol Record Office, *Town Clerk's Letter Book* (05158), October 7 1793.
18. *Minutes of the Proceedings of the Common Council*, Saturday 29th September 1793. (Note that this is incorrectly dated: it should read Sunday 29th) Reference B.R.L. B13065
19. Bohstedt, J., *Riots and Community Politics in England and Wales 1790-1810* (1983), p.202.
20. Harrison M *'To Raise and Dare Resentment': The Bristol Bridge Riot of 1793 Re-Examined*, The Historical Journal 26, 3 (1983) p. 582.
21. *Bonner & Middletons Bristol Journal*, October 5 1793.
22. *Bonner & Middletons Bristol Journal*, October 12 1793.
23. *Bonner & Middletons Bristol Journal*, October 5 1793.
24. B.R.O. Town Clerk's Box 1793.

SEVEN

Poets and pamphleteers

Even if the Corporation's insouciance prevented its administrative incompetence being made public, it did however precipitate the publication of a wide range of unofficial handbills and pamphlets. Although it certainly would have liked to, the Bristol Corporation was not able to silence the press.

Prior to the 18th century the most effective way for the labouring poor to make themselves heard was through the combined voice of the crowd. With the spread of literacy, a range of more sophisticated techniques for political lobbying developed. By the Mid Georgian era a variety of non-violent forms of political pressure were pioneered by such groups as those campaigning for parliamentary reform or the abolition of the slave trade. While the methods of the illiterate labouring poor were intimidation, brute force, riot and arson the new middle-class radicals learnt to exert their influence through petitions, lobbying, meetings and even, in some notable cases, poetry.

Throughout the century a constant stream of broadsheets, tracts and cartoons flowed from the presses across the country. Undoubtedly an irritant to those in authority, the sheer tide of the material made their suppression virtually impossible. And as civil libel actions were not encouraged, writers could sail close to the wind. Indeed, a libel action was only likely to be successful when the offended party was a judge or a magistrate!

For the two weeks following the massacre there was an almost daily output of handbills. Although many were anonymous, judging by their typographical style and content, the handbills came from at least four sources. One of these publishers was even based in London. The publications fall into three very broad categories: first, seriously reasoned pamphlets and broadsheets; second, outright satires and lampoons; and third, poetical ballads[1]. Two local publishers, Robert Rosser, proprietor of the *Bristol Mercury and Universal Advertiser,* and John Rose, the Corporation's most outspoken critic, were both equally forthright in making their opposing views known. While Robert Rosser attempted to publish his tracts behind a veil of anonymity[2], Rose believed that such a smokescreen would be self-defeating and would ultimately weaken his argument. Anyway, given Rose's well-known radical views, he probably felt that his cover would have been quickly blown. Indeed Rose was anxious to be taken seriously and in the introduction to his 16-page 'Impartial History of the Late Disturbances' he disassociated himself from the 'squibs and lampoons, etc. respecting the conduct of the Magistrates...as the subject is too serious to be treated ludicrously'[3].

While Rosser published *'An Impartial History of the Late Riots'*, Rose countered with *'Impartial History of the Late Disturbances'* (The use of the word 'impartial' was the giveaway that both authors had a definite point of view to put forward!) Rosser, an ardent supporter of the Corporation, acknowledged that the high mortality was to be regretted but concluded that 'in the eyes of an impartial person, it appears that they have done no more than their duty". Indeed, Rosser went on to say that had such vigorous action been taken in London in 1780 the Gordon Riots – the most violent riots of the 18th Century – would have been quelled at the outset[4]. Although Rose's description of the 'disturbances' (not 'riot', note) largely concurs with that of Rosser his analysis of the Corporation's role is extremely critical. 'Would not a less rigorous punishment

A Going! A Going! A Going!!

Walk in Ladies and Gentlemen, the *Auction* is juſt going to begin;

A CAPITAL SELECTION OF

BRISTOL WORTHIES,

I ASSURE YE.

Auctioneer.....Ladies and Gentlemen, the firſt Lot I have to offer is Ig*n*ble and Twig Pigeon,—two Perſons; who by a long Practice of the moſt deteſtable Vices have rendered their Names *Infamous* and *deſpicable*; the one is a perfect adept in *lying*,..and the other equally as much in *ſwearing*; and will prove a valuable acquiſtion to their Poſſeſſor, by ſending them to act as occaſional Witneſſes at the Old Bailey:..they are of the Amphibious kind, and can live either on Land or in the Water...Ladies they are ſo innocent you may place them in your Bed-Chamber.

A Lady.....Pray Sir, are not theſe the Gentlemen who ſo wantonly ſported with the Lives of ſo many Citizens on a late occaſion?

Auctioneer.....Yes Madam! but muſt certainly make ſome allowance for Inebriation.

A Gentleman....Twenty Guineas!

Auctioneer..... Thank you Sir,..and if you wiſh to diſpoſe of them *Sir Sampson Wright* will purchaſe them as he is in want of *True Blood Hounds*.

LOT II.....Is R*ss*r the *Pr-nt-r*, or the flying *Mercury*;..Ladies this is a very curious Lot I now offer you; it is difficult to determine which Quality ſhines moſt conſpicuous in this Gentleman, *Ignorance* or *Gluttonny;* as an inſtance of the former, place him on the oppoſite ſide of the Fire to that which he uſually ſits, and he really don't know his Right Hand from his Left...Ladies, this is the Author of a Pamphlet juſt publiſhed, called an *Impartial History* of the late Riots, a Publication made up of "Air of thin Air" throughout the whole of which he proves himſelf a Cat in the Paws of a Monkey...Gentlemen he is a mere *Tool* of *C-rp-r-tre Power*, and to gain a little favor will ſtoop to the moſt abject meaneſs.

Old Lady.....Excuſe me Mr. Auctioneer, my ſight is rather bad, pray is the Lot up Male or Female?

Auctioneer.....It is an *Hermaphrodite* Madam.

A Gentleman.....Forty Shillings!

Auctioneer.....Thank you Sir, though he is worth much more to act as *Pimp* to a *Bawd House*; however I will throw you his companion Tom B*n*s into the Bargain.

LOT III....Mynheer Van H*ll and W*rr*ll,..Gentlemen theſe are appointed by *Lucifer* as his Vicegerents,..they are proof to what a ſtate Villany and Cruelty can arrive too...Treachery and Hipocriſy are their leading Qualities,..and in ſuch repute in Lying, as to become quite proverbial:..they keep a Lodging Houſe for Thieves, and will find you ſpecial Bail for *Wilful Murder!*

A Jew.....Five Guineas!

Auctioneer.....Thank you Sir, and as you bid with ſpirit I give you Jack R*c into the Bargain.

LOT IV.....Lord Bobadil and his *Hounds*, alſo the whole Tribe of Thief Takers, bailiffs and others,..they are a peſt to Community, you ſhall therefore have them Cheap.

A Jew.....Twenty Guineas!

Auctioneer.....It is really too little; why there is that Monſter in Iniquity Joe H*rl*r, a Man fit for *Murder, Treason, Stratagem*, and *Death*, give him a Shilling he'll curſe his Father! he alone is worth twice the Sum;..beſides there is H*mphr**s the *Blood Hound*, commonly called the *Babe of Hell*; and M*rr*ck the *Black Prince of Morocco*.

A Jew.....Fifty Guineas!

Auctioneer.....Sir I am obliged to you and for your Encouragement, I throw you in Bl*nn*c the *Dyer*, alias the *Walking Dung Muxon*.

LOT V. P*lm*r the *Sh-r-ff*, alias *Lucifer's Licentiate*, who have promiſed him as a recompence for his long courſe of *wickedness* to make him *Pike Officer* in the *Realms* of *Perdition*;..alſo Capt. D*v*d, and Symm*nds, who to the B....e Tr-ſt..s acts the *Jackall* or *Lion's Provider*.

A Lady of Pleasure.....Three Guineas!

Auctioneer.....Thank you Madam, they will do any dirty Work, and no doubt will prove excellent *Bullies*.

LOT VI.....M*rg*n the M*y*r,..the Gentleman I now offer to you is perfectly innocent from ſetting the Thames on Fire;..he is no Conjurer as was reported...I aſſure you Ladies and Gentlemen he poſſeſſes many good Qualities, nor did he permit theſe Circumſtances which ſo recently diſtracted this City; but at the continued and preſſing Solicitation of theſe who form the Lots I have juſt ſold to you. He is Charitable, Humane and Generous...the Widow's Petition is not preſented in Vain; nor the Cry of the Fatherleſs of none Effect;..his faults lean to "Virtues Side,"

A Lady.....Twenty Thouſand Guineas!

Auctioneer.....Madam I thank you, and doubt not but you will prove him good and virtuous.

..........Here a Shriek interrupted the Sale, on enquiry it was R*ss*r the *Pr-nt-r*, who declared he had ſeen the Ghoſt of Powell clothed in "Majeſty of Mud"! but it had vaniſhed into "Air, into thin Air."!

Several Ladies fainting;.....and the flying Mercury ſmelling rather ſtrong, the Auctioneer poſtponed the Sale of the Remainder for a few Days.

N. B. During the Sale there was a HORNPIPE in taſte by Paddy B*rk*; and a Minuet by Lieutenant M*xw*ll, and an impure of the Ton.

GOD SAVE THE KING.

[*Price THREE-PENCE.*]

In a popular satirical scenario the principal protagonists of the disturbances are put up for auction. This handbill reveals some of the mood and gossip of the time. Robert Rosser, the printer of the Bristol Mercury and Universal Advertiser, is implicated as the anonymous author of the pro-Corporation booklet 'An Impartial History of the Late Riots'. Rosser is also accused of gluttony and being an hermaphrodite. In contrast, Morgan the Mayor is praised, without any hint of irony, as 'Charitable, Humane and Generous'. (Bristol Reference Library) have done?' he asked. And in a roundabout way Rose raised the question that was on everybody's lips: 'Who gave the order to fire?' Thus he closed by suggesting that the relatives of the deceased should instigate a legal inquiry into the events.

Although Rose and Rosser made some attempt to stick to the facts (as they saw them) many other broadsheets resorted to satire and ridicule. One broadsheet issued from the fictitious 'Cain and Abel Tavern' has the city's surgeons, undertakers and gravediggers giving a vote of thanks to the Corporation for the extra business that had been passed their way. It chillingly invites Corporation members to come forward to be fitted for a new suit from the 'Iron Taylor' which 'will not wear out till the bodies of the persons who wear them are extinct'[5]. In another paper, the city worthies, in a popular satirical scenario, are put up for auction. During this hilarious fictitious sale, which could have come straight out of a Sheridan play, there is an enquiry from the audience about one of the lots (a thinly disguised Robert Rosser):

'Excuse me Mr Auctioneer, my light is rather bad, pray is the lot up male or female?

Auctioneer: 'It is an hermaphrodite, Madam'[6].

If rational argument had little effect on the Corporation and supporters, ridicule at least provided a therapeutic form of revenge.

Though in many cases these handbills are obviously not an accurate reflection of events they do at least give an indication of how people felt about the disturbances. Several themes recur: falsification of accounts by the Bridge Commissioners; accusations of drunkenness among the Corporation and the Militia, and republicanism among the supporters of a general enquiry.

The anonymous writers of these defamatory publications were well aware of the tactics for the evasion of prosecution for libel and usually used pseudonyms or blanked out part of the names. For most readers, however, the targets were blatantly obvious. John Noble was named 'Ignoble' or sometimes 'Mr. 6s.8d.' – a reference the medieval coin, the noble, worth one third of a pound; James Morgan the druggist was called 'Little Jemmy Drug'; Lord Bateman was 'Lord Bobadil', while rather more enigmatically, George Daubeny was given the title 'Twig Pigeon' – a nickname that he had held for many years and was in use when he stood for Parliament in 1784[7].

In their description of the events on 30 September the *London Star* were sure enough of their facts to present a most unflattering report which went so far as to actually name George Daubeny in full:

...Mr Alderman Daubeny, appeared, attended by a numerous posse of constables, after haranguing the people in some of his most refined language, relating a story, and applying its moral...and finding his speeches to no avail, he attacked a man, in a very clean and decent apparel who stood in the most tranquil manner, with his cane, commanding him with all the authority of a magistrate to immediately depart...[8]

Not surprisingly, Daubeny was outraged at this report. He subsequently asked for the Common Council's support to seek the opinion of the Attorney General regarding prosecution for libel. The Common Council duly voted in December 1793 for funds to be made available – though in the end there is no record of any further action being taken[9]. Indeed, if they had pursued this course, surely, all manner of sleeping dogs would have been disturbed.

So what purpose did these pamphlets and broadsheets serve? In the face of the Corporation's intransigence a barrage of satire and ridicule – the verbal equivalent of a Hogarth or Gillray cartoon – was one of the few ways of making an impact on those in authority. In the twenty-first century the effectiveness of a demonstration is judged as much by its media coverage as by the number of people mobilised. Likewise, these pamphlets and broadsheets must have had the scope to influence public opinion. And even if there was no official recourse to justice there was at least some satisfaction in that the accused were reduced to laughing stocks within their own community.

It could also be argued that in tearing away the respectability of authority these publications served as a useful outlet for the release of frustration. Despite the Council's desire for the troubles to go away, the issues were nevertheless brought out and given a good airing.

The shock waves created by the unrest spread far and wide. Some of the ladies (and gentlemen) of Bristol's leisured drawing-room society were even inspired to present their thoughts in rhyming couplets:

'While Bullets flew – from street to street –
Leaving no moment to retreat.
But winging through the smoke and fire
Many numbers groan! bleed! and expire!'[10]

(This was the only recorded female voice to be heard in connection with the Bristol Bridge 'riot'.)

In a similar poetical vein, but even more blood-curdlingly explicit, was 'A Retrospect of the Tragical Events which Lately

Oct. 1, 1793.

Cain and Abel TAVERN,

Near BRISTOL BRIDGE.

At a Meeting of Delegates aſſembled, it was decreed as follows:

THE SURGEONS of this City return their ſincere Thanks to *George Pigeon*, Eſq. (originally from *France*); and to a NOBLE *Six-and-Eight-Pence* (of *Liſbon* extraction), for their kind Efforts in giving them further Experience, which before was only *caſual* or *natural* till Monday Night laſt; when they were called repeatedly to *Military Caſes*: which they preſume have done Credit to their Skill.

THE UNDERTAKERS who are employed in conſequence of the Exertions of their *noble* Friends on Monday Night would be wanting in Gratitude, not to come forward on this public Occaſion to acknowledge their Obligations for the ſame. And ſincerely hope, the Lives of Perſons ſo eminently diſtinguiſhed for their good *Qualities*, may be ſpared to exert themſelves till *two* other Occaſions offer to revive their Employ, *viz*. the Erection of a *Baſtile*, and the making a *Floating River*.

THE GRAVE-DIGGERS (unanimous) of the ſame Opinion, ſincerely wiſh, the Iron Hand of Death will ſpare the GUILTY, till the preſent Hurry of Buſineſs, on Account of the Orders received ſince laſt Monday Night, is executed;—but rather than not oblige *two particular Friends*, will willingly forego the Emoluments of the Digging Trade, by accepting *Thirteen-pence-half-penny* per Head inſtead.

THE RELATIVES of the Deceaſed and Wounded cannot offer their Services till the Murdered are buried out of their Sight; but if thoſe two particular Friends of the Deceaſed, ſhould have injured their Cloaths, &c. they are very ready to employ their *Iron* Taylor, to compleatly meaſure them for a New Suit, which will not wear out till the Bodies of the Perſons who occupy them are extinct.

A Deputation of the peaceable Inhabitants of this City now handed,

It was unanimouſly agreed,

To petition the Civil Power, that, notwithſtanding whatever might be the Severity of the enſuing Winter, they may be protected from every FIRE, and particularly from thoſe Orders which may be given to FIRE LOW.—

And laſtly, they requeſt that they may have Liberty in future to remove the Dead: and not whilſt there is Life, have their Friends thrown over the Bridge.

Signed by Order of the Meeting,

George Pigeon,
Noble John.

Cain & Abel Tavern, a satirical handbill. A delegation of surgeons, undertakers and gravediggers voice their thanks for the extra work they have been given. The relatives of the deceased make the chilling offer to George Pigeon (George Daubeny) and Noble John (John Noble) of an iron suit 'which will not wear out till the bodies of the persons who occupy them are extinct'. Reference is also made to the order to the troops to 'fire low', and the unsubstantiated stories of bodies being thrown over the bridge. (Bristol Reference Library)

Happened in Bristol' containing the stanza:

'Loud shrieks, and groans, resounded in the air;
And every mind was filled with black despair:
And Bozley's House was smeared with human brains!'[11]

Not all of the poetical ballads were totally vacuous, however. One of Bristol's literati, the semi anonymous 'GJ' even went so far as to take the bold political stance of supporting the call for an official enquiry. Yet this barrage of condemnation from all quarters fell on deaf ears; the Council steadfastly resisted all attempts to set up a public enquiry. In the face of such intransigence an anonymous handbill issued one week after the tragic events accused the magistracy of awing the people into 'silence and submission' and suggested that: 'some sensible, humane and generous citizens form themselves into a society of investigation, and if necessary prosecution!'[12] As the days went by this seemed about the only viable option left.

'SUSPICIOUS AND PREGNANT WITH THE MOST ALARMING MISCHIEF'

Eventually it was Dr. Edward Long Fox, a physician who had been called out to treat the dying and wounded on the night of the massacre, who took it upon himself to lead the unofficial enquiry. Born in Falmouth in 1761, Doctor Fox had been elected as a physician to the Bristol Infirmary in 1786[13]. The Doctor was a man of great ability and enthusiasms. He inspired extremes of emotion in those who knew him. To his supporters he was the mildest and fairest of men; to his opponents he was a dangerous promoter of

PLAIN TRUTH.

ABOUT Thirty-four Years ago it was found neceſſary to build a new Bridge, Commiſſioners were appointed and an Act obtained for that Purpoſe: A Tax was laid on Houſes and Shipping, and a Toll on Carriages and Cattle for defraying the Expence. This Buſineſs, though of the utmoſt Conſequence to the Intereſt of the Public, continued many Years without a Committee or any regular Settlement of the Accounts: nay in this State did they remain till the Truſtees were obliged by Law to publiſh them, which, agreeable to the act, they ought to have done Yearly, *there being a Clauſe expreſsly to that Purpoſe.*

In the account thus *forced* from them, they credited the Public for Twenty-ſix Years at about £.1200 per Annum on the Average.

The laſt Rentor, who collected the Tolls himſelf, has in one Year received £.3000; by this *Fact* it appears that there have been about £.46,800 more collected on the Toll *only* than the Public were ever before acquainted with.—This being the *Fact* reſpecting the Tolls, there is every reaſon to believe that *nefarious Practices, in proportion to Opportunity,* have been committed in all the other Departments of this great Public Concern.

That this Burden might have been taken off at leaſt ten Years paſt, and with it a prevention to all the late dreadful Effects of bad Managers and plundering Dependants, is too clear in every honeſt Mind to need any further proof.

Let Oblivion caſt her Veil over the wanton Cruelty ſuffered by our unfortunate Brother Citizens, but let not their Aſhes be polluted by the *Infamy, Slander, and Falſhood of thoſe Proud, Inſolent, Rapacious, and Cruel Wretches, who are themſelves the very Slaves of Vice.

God save the King, and our Liberties,
From Hypocrites, Thieves, Petty TYRANTS,
And all vain MONSTERS!!

*In hopes to ſanction the late Murders, and (if poſſible) wipe off the foul Stain of BLOOD thoſe little Creatures, with all the artful Falſhood that Hell itſelf could invent, have meanly inſinuated that the *Citizens* wiſhed for a Revolution, and a Mob Government.

Pitiful Subterfuge! Immortal JUSTICE is not thus deceived by KNAVES and FOOLS!!!

N. B. No Citizen has been ſhot by a Soldier ſince the Days of OLIVER CROMWELL, till the late drunken and violent Maſſacre, committed on an unarmed Multitude.

ABOUT ONE HUNDRED KILLED AND WOUNDED.

'Plain Truth'. An anonymously produced handbill. Despite any real evidence, there was a rumour of a republican plot to undermine those in authority. Such talk, which played on the fears of the citizens, was extremely difficult to disprove. (Bristol Reference Library)

republican principles[14]. Whatever their viewpoint, few could have denied the courage and dedication – albeit, according to his critics, misguided – of a man who was willing to take on the might of the Corporation.

The enterprising Dr. Fox was one of a new breed who, though not born into the ruling elite, actively aspired to be involved in the political process. During the latter part of the eighteenth century dissenting religious groups such as the Quakers, the Methodists and the Baptists began to develop strategies for asserting their rights and implementing religious reform. Dissenters, who in theory were barred from political life – though this certainly was not the case in Bristol – insisted that there should be toleration for 'all modes of thinking'. 'A free constitution,' wrote the political reformer Joseph Priestly, in 1773 'should not deprive itself the services of any man of ability and integrity on account of his religious opinions any more than on account of the colour of his hair'[15].

The dissenting groups well understood the basic dilemma of political protest. As Bristol's former MP, Edmund Burke, wrote

'if the people are riotous, nothing is to be done for them on account of their evil dispositions. If they are obedient and loyal, nothing is to be done for them, because their being quiet and contented, is proof that they feel no grievance.'[16]

During the 1780s the dissenting religious groups devised new, more peaceful, and indeed ultimately more effective, forms of protest.

What was novel about the approach of the Quakers and Methodists was that they looked for ways of working *within* the political structure to effect permanent change. This included such tactics as the setting up of public petitions linked to the well-researched and co-ordinated lobbying of those with political clout. By the 1790s such new processes of protest had already borne limited fruit. For example, during the 1780s Bristol's Quakers – many of whom had prospered well over the years from the triangular trade – took the bold stance of boycotting the slave trade. Although the slave trade was in the process of being wound down, the Quakers' rejection of it was still a major step to take, for in effect, they were cutting at the very heart of Bristol's wealth. By November 1786 Bristol's Quakers were able to report that with one exception – a Friend who had recently retired from the West Indies and was still trying to sell his property – none of its members were directly involved in the slave trade[17].

By January 1788 the abolitionists, led by Joseph Harford, had substantial support from such figures as the Deans of Bristol and Gloucester, as well as a number of prominent merchants including, in a rare fit of compassion, Harford's banking partner, George Daubeny. (Predictably Daubeny's moment of compassion was short-lived. He subsequently changed his mind and withdrew his backing. Indeed he was soon to be a member of the Merchant Venturer's committee set up to defend the traffic[18].) During the following month a petition, initially originated in Manchester, for signatures (men only) of those who supported the Anti Slave Trade Movement was set up in Bristol's Guildhall[19].

So, Dr. Fox was not embarking upon entirely unchartered waters when he wrote to James Morgan on 21 October 1793 suggesting that, as Mayor, he should chair a public meeting at the Guildhall to discuss recent events. This must have set alarm bells ringing, for the Mayor replied with almost indecent haste on the same day that it had been unanimously decided by Council members that he should neither chair a meeting nor allow the Guildhall to be used for this purpose[20]. As a public enquiry was the last thing that the Corporation wanted the motives of Dr. Fox – now nicknamed 'Jacobin Fox' – and his colleagues were dismissed out of hand as being 'suspicious and pregnant with the most alarming mischief'. To be sure of their ground Dr. Fox and his colleagues quickly sought expert legal advice from London as to the legality of any public assembly to investigate the *causes* of the disturbances. Mr. Piggott from Lincoln's Inn pronounced that such a meeting was not unlawful so long as it was conducted in a 'quiet and peaceable manner'[21].

As he was denied the use of the Guildhall and the cooperation of the Council, Dr. Fox subsequently booked Coopers Hall in King Street for a public meeting at 10 am on 29 October. Three days later the booking was refused. Undaunted, Mr. Young's warehouse in Lewins Mead was secured. Again, the offer was soon withdrawn. The unseen hand of the Council was undoubtedly working to frustrate the setting up of any enquiry.

In the absence of a public meeting Fox sought to establish a small working committee to advance the enquiry forward. The first meeting of the seven man committee was held in Baldwin Street on 20 November 1793. Although the committee was not officially recognised, the importance of establishing formal procedures was well understood and a long list of terms of reference for the enquiry was drawn up; minutes were to be taken and it was resolved that 'no subject of a political nature should be introduced'. Reflecting their fears of subterfuge, they purchased a cabinet for the secure storage of all the committee's notes. The key was to be held by committee members and then passed on. The cabinet was only ever to be opened in the presence of all the committee members. Meetings lasting two hours were to be held twice weekly, on Monday and

Thursday starting 'at seven by St Stephen's clock'.

They were all well aware of the contentiousness of their enquiry during such troubled times and in an attempt to legitimise their findings they sought to appoint a solicitor. Their first choice, Mr. Payne refused their invitation but their second choice, Mr. Woodforde, accepted. Their intentions could well be misconstrued. As we have seen, the label 'Republican' was a useful smear for anyone who wished to challenge the status quo. The members must have realised the perils of the task they were embarking upon. They risked being socially ostracized and even personal physical danger.

For three long months members of the committee tirelessly sought to gather evidence. For two evenings a week they trudged the dark winter streets seeking witnesses, recording their testimony and reporting back to the committee. Some who gave evidence – often relatives of those who had been directly involved – were remarkably frank. Those in positions of authority, however, were usually more guarded and on several occasions committee members recounted their view that they were not being presented with the full story. It seemed as if the Council had closed ranks with a conspiracy of silence.

The committee unveiled a number of weaknesses in the chaotic system of local policing. First of all it was not clear whether all the local constables had actually been summoned on the Saturday night, as orders were issued by word of mouth rather than in writing, as was the usual case. And then, to make matters worse, a number of constables who did receive their orders refused to obey them. Three of the chief constables were out – or claimed to be – even at the late hour of 11 pm, whilst Mr. Bevan, the chief constable of St Thomas Ward, blatantly ignored the magistrates, orders and chose to sit at home[22]. On the other hand, in several cases, those who did attempt to attend responded in a far from responsible and authoritative manner. Mr. Edgar, Chief Constable of St Michael's Ward, arriving at the bridge without his staff of office, decided to join the crowd as a spectator rather than an officer of the peace[23]. In fairness to Mr. Edgar, although other constables voiced their disquiet at the use of the military, he was one of the few people interviewed who considered their presence not merely unwise, but illegal and was thus anxious to disassociate himself from the consequences.

The committee agreed that one of the most crucial facts to establish was the identity of the person who gave the orders to fire, the person who should take ultimate responsibility for the massacre. It has to be said that it was quite remarkable that such a significant element in events should, at this stage, still be clouded by mystery. Even though one of the soldiers was heard to boast that he was ready for a reward to say who had given the order[24] the culprit remained protected. One witness, John Hannam, claimed he heard Lord Bateman give the order to 'fire low, breast high'. But as Hannam was at the top of the High Street at the time, his account was less than credible[25]. William James said that he heard John Noble give the order for the second volley[26].

In the end the finger of guilt seemed to point to a most unlikely culprit. Vining, a broker from Thomas Street 'speaks pretty positively' that Horler, the Mayor's Secretary gave an order to fire[27]; this evidence was further corroborated by a Mr. Langsbridge[28]. Yet, in reality this whole train of investigation was immaterial. Horler was in no position to be issuing such orders on his own authority. One can only surmise that on that fateful night, when the militia marched with muskets primed from the Guildhall down to the bridge, they had already been well-briefed by the magistrates. Thus, when the soldiers took up their firing positions and Horler issued the order to fire he was setting into action a battle plan that had already been agreed upon. Horler was, in fact, no more culpable than Daubeny's 'bugle boy'.

The committee was wasting its time seeking out the person who gave the order to fire. They should have realised that the responsibility rested in general with the magistrates, and in particular with the chief magistrate, Mayor James Morgan. Poor unfortunate James Morgan! By all accounts he was a well-meaning and honourable man – yet it was his misfortune to be in the wrong place at the wrong time. To anyone of the least observation it was not the mild mannered Morgan who was in control over those fateful days. It was plainly obvious to all and sundry, including theanonymous correspondent to Prime Minister Pitt, that although James Morgan was legally in charge it was, in fact, George Daubeny and John Noble who were giving the orders. In the memorable phrase of one observer Morgan was merely 'a cat's paw in the hands of a monkey'.

Unfortunately for Morgan, the ultimate responsibility for law and order in the city rested with the Mayor – in this case, himself. Having gathered their evidence the next question was what to do with it. After three months the committee sought advice from Mr. Vaughan, a legal expert, as to how they should proceed next. Vaughan advised that 'a committee as such cannot bring a prosecution' and that it would be up to an individual to take matters forward. While Vaughan thought that the report of the committee's transactions would be valuable he cautioned that they should be very discreet in the way they presented their evidence 'for no libel is held to be so great as when reflecting on a magistrate in the execution of his office'. Referring to the recent battle of the broadsheets Vaughan felt that 'crime should be prosecuted rather than published'[29]. In other words, if they had proof of criminal mismanagement they should go ahead and do something about it. Even so, Vaughan's final grave warning was that unless the committee had 'very complete proof' prosecution should not be 'commenced on any account'.

This was the crunch, for although the committee had gathered numerous vignettes of evidence the overall picture was still vague. Most important of all was the fact that no city leaders had been interviewed. And then again, could those who had supplied damning evidence to the committee of enquiry be relied upon to repeat their claims in public in a court of law?

As a last ditch effort the committee considered offering a reward for further evidence, but on reflection decided that such a course of action could jeopardise their impartiality. Rewards could be equated with bribes or, even worse, the unscrupulous could be encouraged to concoct fictitious testimony.

Although the minute book indicates no lack of enthusiasm the committee's enquiry came to a sudden and unforeseen halt. The entry for 3 March 1794 records, as usual, committee members, reporting back on the evidence they had gathered since the previous meeting. This was however, the last time the record book was used. There were no further entries. What had happened? Why was the committee so hastily abandoned? One can only speculate, but there must surely have been a further meeting when the group decided to terminate their investigation. Perhaps, they had taken the advice of Mr. Vaughan, and seeing no clear way forward, had abandoned their crusade. Yet, for a group that had been so thorough, and had set out clear procedures for operation, it was out of character not to tie up loose ends and record their final resolutions. Maybe, and there is no hard evidence to support this suspicion, more sinister pressures were afoot? Were the bullies of the Corporation, in some unknown way, exerting threats that could no longer be ignored?

Or perhaps, with the growing realisation of the naivety of their aim and the impossibility of indicting the likes of George Daubeny, together with the expense and futility of taking on the might of the Corporation, they had simply lost hope.

So, less than five months after the disturbances, all attempts to bring the authorities responsible for the massacre to justice had failed. Despite the barrage of critical broadsheets and pamphlets, the clamour for a public meeting and the investigations of the unofficial committee of enquiry Morgan, Bengough, Daubeny and the rest of the chamber remained unscathed. In short, following one of the worst civilian massacres of eighteenth century Britain no one had been brought to trial, nor had any named person been officially implicated.

'GIVE 'EM BRISTOL BRIDGE'

In fact, the hysterical behaviour of Bristol's Corporation gave a taste of a forthcoming national repression of civil rights and the beginning of a bleak period for English freedom. By the end of 1795, as the country became increasingly embroiled in war with Revolutionary France, Pitt's Government shook the very bedrock of liberty by suspending the Habeas Corpus Act. Additionally, in an attempt to stamp out any form of protest, legislation outlawed meetings of over fifty people and extended the law of high treason to cover the excitement of contempt of the King, criticism of the constitution or, even, of the Government[30].

Predictably there was disquiet right across the country over the so called 'gagging bills'. It comes as no surprise to find none other than Dr. Edward Long Fox, who had obviously recovered from his

Bristol Bridge in quieter times. The toll is no longer collected and the toll-houses are let as shops. (City of Bristol Museum and Art Gallery)

set-back of the previous year, leading the local protests against Pitt's ruthless repression[31].

In some aspects the actions of the Corporation in Bristol during the autumn of 1793 could be seen as a precursor to this national democratic step backwards – although in Bristol they were motivated by a different, and perhaps, less noble aspect of self-protection.

As we have seen while Bristol Corporation members escaped prosecution they did not, however, avoid widespread censure. The Corporation's reputation, which at the best of times was poor, was diminished even further. For several years after the violence of the autumn of 1793, the Council appeared discredited and demoralised; it was forced to introduce a series of fines for non-attendance at meetings, whilst in 1794 the first two choices for Mayor refused to serve[32]. Even so the regime of Bristol's arrogant elite was to continue as such for nearly another 40 years. Matters were eventually brought to a head by the Bristol Riots of 1831 when the populace undoubtedly did go on the rampage. For three days the city was at the mercy of the mob: the Bishop's Palace was raided; prisoners were released from the New Gaol on the Cut; and the Mansion House along with many other residences in Queen Square was looted and set alight. Only after mounted dragoons charged through the streets slashing freely with their sabres was order restored[33]. Indeed, the country was so shocked by Bristol's three days of anarchy that the national campaign for Parliamentary Reform was further hastened along by the disturbances. With the Reform Act of 1832 the Corporation at last became more accountable. The Merchant Venturers, meanwhile, their power undiminished, quietly retreated into the shadows[34].

The Bridge 'Riots' and the events surrounding them can be seen to epitomise all that was worst in eighteenth century Bristol. The city was to be haunted by this moment of murder for many years to come. Nearly one hundred years later, when Victorian youths wished to taunt those in authority, they would hark back to those tragic days and raise the chilling cry of defiance 'Give 'em Bristol Bridge'[35]. Despite all the attempts of the Corporation to play-down events on the Bridge, the massacre of 1793 had nevertheless become firmly etched into local folklore.

Notes

1. Manson, M., *Pamphlets, Broadsheets and the Bristol Bridge 'Riot' of 1793* in The Local Historian Volume 25 (1995), no.2, pp.66-76.
2. His identity – along with other proclivities – was exposed in the satirical leaflet *'Capital Selection of Bristol Worthies'* – Bristol Reference Library B. 13081.
3. Rose, J. *Impartial History of the Late Disturbances in The City of Bristol* (Bristol 1793), p. 2
4. Rosser, p.16.
5. Cain & Abel Tavern, (Bristol 1793) Bristol Reference Library B.13081.
6. *Capital Selection of Bristol Worthies* (Undated) Bristol Reference Library B.13081.
7. The origin of this nickname is uncertain. I'd be pleased to hear anyone's ideas about its derivation. M.M.
8. *London Star,* October 4 1793.
9. B.R.O. *Minutes of the Proceedings of the Common Council* 1791-6, p.256-7.
10. *Thoughts Occasioned by the Proceedings on Bristol Bridge – by a Lady,* undated B.R.L. B.13105
11. Anon., *A Retrospect of the Tragical Events which Lately Happened in Bristol* (Bristol, undated), B.R.L. B.25368.
12. Anonymous broadsheet, *'Inquisition for Blood shall be made'* B.R.L. B.13077.
13. Munroe Smith, G., *History of the Bristol Royal Infirmary* (Bristol 1917) pp. 474-477.
14. 'A.W." *A Letter to Edward Long Fox, MD* (Eight page pamphlet dated: Bristol December 1795.) p.6.
15. Blackburn R., *The Overthrow of Colonial Slavery 1776-1848* (1988), p.135-8.
16. Gilmour,I., *Riot, Risings and Revolution* (London 1992) p.16.
17. Marshall, P., *The Anti-Slave Trade Movement in Bristol in the 18th Century,* ed. P. McGrath (Newton Abbot 1972) p.187.
18. Latimer, J., *The History of the Society of Merchant Venturers of the City of Bristol* (1903), p.185.
19. Marshall, P., p.194.
20. *The Town Clerk's Correspondence Book* B.R.O. 05158 contains a note requesting that Dr Fox along with Messrs Godwin, Powell and Weaver attend the Mansion House. I could find no record of what transpired at the meeting – if it happened.

21. *Note from A Piggott, Lincoln's Inn* 26th October 1793. BCRL B.13089.
22. Committee, p.26.
23. Committee, p.71.
24. Committee, p.34.
25. Committee, p.41.
26. Committee, p.46.
27. Committee, p.25.
28. Committee, p.26.
29. Committee, p.59.
30. Wells, R. *Insurrection: the British Experience* (Alan Sutton, Gloucester 1986) p. 23.
31. 'A.W.', *A Letter to Edward Long Fox, M.D.*, 8 page pamphlet dated Bristol, Dec. 11, 1795.
32. Latimer, J., *Annals of Eighteenth Century Bristol* p. 507
33. Manson, M., *Bristol: Beyond the Bridge,* (1988) pp.75-8.
34. Latimer, J., *The History of the Society of Merchant Venturers on the City of Bristol*(1903), p.243.
35. Hunt W. Bristol (London 1887) p. 202.

Afterword

Henry Bengough (d. 1818)

By the time of his death, Bengough's involvement with the Bristol Bridge massacre was well behind him. Indeed, although he was a Unitarian, he was so proud of his connections with the Corporation that he made a special plea to be buried in the Lord Mayor's Chapel. He left a substantial sum of money to fund the establishment of Bengough's Almshouse on St. Michael's Hill.

George Daubeny (1742 – 1806)

Unscathed by his involvement with the events of 1793 Daubeny continued to play a leading role in the affairs of the city right until his death in 1806. He was buried in the family crypt in St James's church.

Edward Long Fox (1761 – 1835)

Dr. Fox eventually became well known as an authority on lunacy and was one of the first people to treat the mentally ill in a humane manner. He built his own asylum at Brislington where he went to live in 1806. In 1816 he resigned from his job at the Infirmary and devoted himself to his special subject. In 1814 the poet Samuel Taylor Coleridge is said to have considered attendance at Dr. Fox's asylum in order to help him in his attempt to overcome opium addiction. He became so famous that he was called to Windsor to advise on King George IIIs long-term insanity. Despite his achievements, Dr Fox was to say that his association with the committee of enquiry prejudiced his career as a medical man and created enemies for life[1].

Wintour Harris (d. 1818)

Harris was appointed City Chamberlain (akin to a treasurer), the highest paid official on the Corporation. When he died in 1818, he was overspent in office by £5,000.

John Noble (d. 1826)

Noble continued to make expensive official trips to London (where coincidently his son worked in the Home Office). He moved to London in 1806 but remained an Alderman of Bristol until his death in 1826.

James Morgan (d. 1794)

Just ten weeks after his term in office as mayor had finished the following brief note appeared in the Bristol papers. 'Sunday last, died at his house in Great George Street, James Morgan Esq, late Mayor of Bristol. He was 49'[2].

John Rose (d. 1816?)

The Bristol literary scene experienced a brief but dramatic flowering in 1795 with the arrival of Samuel Taylor Coleridge in the city. Bristol was the scene of one of the great moments of English Literature when, in the Pinney household in Great George Street, Coleridge was first introduced to William Wordsworth[3]. Coleridge's brief stay in Bristol injected an energy into the city's literary life that had never been experienced before – or since. Rose continued his business as bookseller and printer until his death. He died 'the wrong side of 50'[4].

Sam Worrall (d.1821)

A man of substantial wealth, among his business interests he was the official distributor of stamps in Bristol. He owned land in Clifton – hence Worral Road. He mixed in high circles and was known to be a frequent guest of the Prince Regent at Carlton House in London. The Worral family had a brief period of national fame when they adopted, until she was exposed as a fake, the mysterious 'Princess Caribou'.

Declared bankrupt in 1818 due to the failure of the Tolzey Bank, of which he was a partner. Worral consequently had to resign as secretary to the Council – he was however awarded a substantial annuity of £4,005. He was buried at Almondsbury, where his life is commemorated by a simple plaque in the south aisle of the parish church.

Bristol Bridge

And finally, what of Bristol Bridge? Although the bridge was extended in Victorian times the superstructure of James Bridges's bridge remains today substantially as it was in 1769. The widening of the east side of the bridge in 1861 and the west side in 1873 required the destruction of the four toll houses[6]. The distinctive balustrade and coping stones were also taken down and subsequently transported to Kings Weston House, just north of Bristol. Today, a few metres away from Vanbrugh's great house, the finely worked coping stones are clearly visible lying ignominiously amongst other rubble in the undergrowth.

Notes

1. *Letter from Edwin Fox to Francis Fox*, BRL B13064
2 F.F.J. 20/12/1794.
3. Holmes R., *Coleridge - Early Visions* (1990) p.92.
4. Lamoine G., *Notes on Bristol's Literary Circle 1794-98.* (1973), B.R.L. B.26474.
5. Latimer J *Annals of Nineteenth Century Bristol* (Bristol 1887) p. 85.
6. Latimer, p.385.

Select Bibliography

PRIMARY SOURCES

Bristol Record Office

Common Council Proceedings 1793

Correspondence Boxes of Town Clerk 1792 & 1793

Quarter Sessions Box 1793

Bristol Royal Infirmary Admissions Records

Town Clerk's Letter Book, ref. 05158

Bristol Reference Library

Braikenridge Collection, Vol 111. 1 p 473–9 Bristol Central Reference Library (BCRL).

George Catcott Collection BCRL B.4985

Bristol Gazette & Public Advertiser – relevant sections bound in with B13065.

Felix Farley's Bristol Journal – 1793 bound copies & microfilm available.

Mardon Collection, BCRL B.11539.

Minutes of the Committee for Investigating the Bridge Affairs BCRL B13065.

SECONDARY SOURCES

Atherton, H.M. *Political Prints of the Age of Hogarth* (Oxford University Press, 1974).

Barret, W., *The History and Antiquities of Bristol* (Bristol 1789).

Blackburn, R., *The Overthrow of Colonial Slavery 1776-1848* (London,Verso,1988)

Buchanan, R.A., *The Industrial Archaeology of Bristol* (Bristol Branch of the

Historical Association 1967).

Bohstedt, J., *Riots and Community Politics in England & Wales, 1790-1810* (Harvard 1983).

Coleman, J., *Against tbe State* (London, BBC Books, 1990).

Colley, L., *Britons - Forging the Nation 1707–1837* (London,Pimlico, 1994).

Cunliffe, B., Bath (Gloucester, Alan Sutton, 1986).

Dyck, I. (ed.) *Citizen of the World: Essays of Thomas Paine* (London, C. Helm, 1987).

Evans, J., *A Chronological Outline of the History of Bristol* (London, 1825).

Foot, M. & Kramnick, I., *Thomas Paine Reader* (London, Penguin,1987).

Gilmour, I., *Riots, Risings and Revolution* (London, Pimlico, 1992).

Harrison, M., *'To Raise and Dare Resentment': the Bristol Bridge Riot of 1793* Reexamined, Historical Journal 26, 3 (1983) pp. 557–585.

Hey, D., *The Oxford Companion to Local and Family History* (Oxford, 1996).

Holmes, R., *Coleridge: Early Visions* (London, Penguin, 1990).

Hunt, W., *Bristol* (London, 1887).

Ibbetson, J., Laporte and Hassel, J., *A Picturesque Guide to Bath, Bristol Hotwells, the River Avon and the Adjacent Country* (London, 1793).

Jones, D., *A History of Clifton* (Chichester, Phillimore, 1992).

Jones, P.D., *The Bristol Bridge Riot and its antecedents: Eighteenth Century Perceptions of the Crowd,* Journal of British Studies, XlX, 2 (1980) pp.74–92.

Ison, W., *The Georgian Buildings of Bristol* (London, Faber & Faber, 1952).

Latimer, J., *Annals of 18th Century Bristol* (Bristol, 1893).

Latimer, J., *Annals of 19th Century Bristol* (Bristol, 1887).

Latimer, J., *The History of the Society of Merchant Venturers of the City of Bristol* (Bristol, 1903).

Little, B., *The City & County of Bristol* (London, 1954).

Maclnnes, C.M.,*A Gateway of Empire* (Newton Abbot 1968).

Maclnnes, C.M. & Whittard, W.F. *Bristol & Its Adjoining Counties* (Bristol, 1955).

Marcy, P.T., *Bristol's Roads and Communications on the Eve of the Industrial Revolution*

(Bristol and Gloucestershire Archaeological Society, Vol 87, 1968).
Manson, M., *Bristol: Beyond the Bridge* (Bristol, Redcliffe, 1988).
Marshall, P., *The Anti-Slave Trade Movement In Bristol In the 18th Century* edited by McGrath, P. (Newton Abbot, 1972)
Matthews, W., *The New History of Bristol or the Complete Guide and Bristol Directory* (Bristol, 1793).
Moore, J.S., *Avon Local History Handbook* (Chichester, Phillimore, 1979).
Pevsner, N., *The Buildings of England - North Somerset and Bristol* (London, Penguin,1958).
Ralph, E., *Government of Bristol 1373–1973* (Bristol, 1974).
Rude, G., *The Crowd in History* (London, Lawrence Wishart, 1981).
Rude, G., *Revolutionary Europe 1783–1815* (London,Fontana, 1964).
Seyer, S., *Memoirs of Bristol* (Bristol 1812-23).
Schama, S., *Citizens* (London, Penguin Books, 1989).
Thompson, E.P., *The Making of the English Working Class* (London, Pelican,1979).
Underdown, P.T., *Bristol and Burke* (Bristol 1961).
Wells, R., *Insurrection: The British Experience 1795–1803* (Gloucester, Alan Sutton, 1986).
Witt, C., *Bristol Fine Wares 1670–1970* (Bristol 1980).
Witt C., *Introducing Bristol Glass* (Bristol, 1984).

Computer Databases
A New Bristol Bibliography (Bristol Historical Database Project, University of the West of England, Bristol, 1996).
The Society of Merchant Venturers (Bristol Historical Database Project, University of the West of England, Bristol, 1995).

Index